As you read through the in[timate conversations of Isabelle] Joye, who is in pursuit of [a deeper relationship with the Lord Jesus] Christ—you get the distinct feeling that you are eavesdropping on a very personal conversation between the awesome creator of heaven and earth and his child Isabelle, who is totally captivated by her Heavenly Father and is hanging off every word that he says. As you travel with her on this adventure, you are going to be challenged to have the same intimate relationship that she has with Jesus, and at the same time pick up some keys and insight to building that relationship that will prepare you for his return. Isabelle has released these private moments with God in obedience to his request, and I believe you will be greatly blessed as you read the pages of this book. People can give you things, but nobody can give you an encounter with God; nobody can give you a history or story with God. Isabelle has shared hers!

Apostle Steven Davis, Perth, Western Australia
Founder of Dream Life Church; author of
In Pursuit of the Call **and** ***Your Dream Is in the House***

Isabelle has, in this book, helped us to understand what a dynamic "quiet time" really looks like. Although written in a simple and easy-to-read manner, the conversation is both intense and penetrating. There seems to be no religious façade in this, as Isabelle describes her struggles and victories.

I believe this will turn out to be a helpful tool in the hands of Christ-followers who desire to inject passion into their prayer life and walk with the Lord. This book is practical, and the experience shared, relatable. I highly recommend it to all believers.

Dr. Joseph Obisesan
Pastor, HillCity Church, Western Australia

Purify my heart

A Dialogue with Jesus

by

Isabelle Joye

Purify My Heart: A Dialogue with Jesus
Copyright © 2020 by Isabelle Joye

Published by Deep River Books
Sisters, Oregon
www.deepriverbooks.com

All rights reserved. No part of this book may be reproduced or transmitted in any form or by any means, electronic or mechanical, including photocopying and recording, or by any information storage and retrieval system, without permission in writing from the publisher.

Unless otherwise indicated, all Scripture quotations are taken from from the THE HOLY BIBLE, NEW INTERNATIONAL VERSION® NIV®. Copyright © 1973, 1978, 1984 by International Bible Society®. Used by permission. All rights reserved worldwide.

Scripture quotations marked GNT have been taken from the Good News Translation® (Today's English Version, Second Edition). Copyright © 1976 American Bible Society. All rights reserved.

Scripture quotations marked NLT are taken from the *Holy Bible*, New Living Translation, copyright © 1996, 2004, 2015 by Tyndale House Foundation. Used by permission of Tyndale House Publishers, Inc., Carol Stream, Illinois 60188. All rights reserved.

Scripture quotations marked KJV are taken from the King James Version. Public domain.

ISBN—13: 9781632695291
Library of Congress Control Number: 2020909669

Printed in the USA
2020—First Edition
29 28 27 26 25 24 23 22 21 20 10 9 8 7 6 5 4 3 2 1

Cover Design by Robin Black, Inspirio Design

Dedication

I dedicate this book to my late mother, Lavinia May, who lovingly and unselfishly dedicated her life to her husband and nine children.

Most of all I thank my Lord and Savior Jesus Christ for love and encouragement.
I dearly pray that he will be honored by all who read this book.

Thank You, Lord

How great You are!

Table of Contents

Introduction 11
Preface. 13
1. You Found Me 15
2. Christian Growth 19
3. Whittling 25
4. Clinging to You. 29
5. All Things Work Together for Good 35
6. Glorious Savior 39
7. Sin 45
8. Your Love 51
9. Overcoming Temptation. 57
10. The Time for Salvation 63
11. Transparency. 69
12. Victor 75
13. Forgiveness 79
14. Walking in Love 85

15. Turn the Other Cheek. 91
16. The Judge 95
17. Eternity. 101
18. Purify My Heart 105
19. Ministry 109
20. Security. 115
21. Money. 119
22. Intercession. 125
23. Eyes on You. 131
24. Wider Intercession 137
25. Significance. 143
26. Busyness 147
27. Healing. 151
28. Instructions 155
29. Overcoming Self. 161
30. Our Source, Our Sacrifice. 167
31. One Look at You. 173
32. Obedience. 179
33. Blind. 185
34. Relinquishment. 191
35. Reassurance. 197
36. Thoughts. 203

37. My Creator 209
38. Christmas 215
39. Pride 219
40. Baptism of Fire 225
41. Storms. 231
42. Nothing Alien 237
43. Ideal 243
44. Your Purpose. 249
45. Radiant Light 255
46. Second Coming. 261
47. Urgency. 267
48. Judgment 273
49. The Word 279
50. Worldwide Fellowship. 285
51. Praise. 291
52. Happiness 297
Endnotes. 301
Acknowledgments. 303

Introduction

As one of nine children from a jubilant farming family, my early life was one of enchanting memories of happy and joyous times together. Alas, although I am now widowed, there are still the joys of three lovely children and seven beautiful grandchildren who I love unconditionally.

This book was not written to be published. It originated as a prayer diary to Jesus into which I wrote my prayers over the years, revealing to him my innermost thoughts and desires. The idea to publish came from a man on Christian TV, who said that God, in a vision, told him he wished the world to be saturated with Christian books, as many people today do not read the Bible. Immediately I thought to myself, "I don't know how to write a book." Instantaneously a thought came to mind: "You *have* a book—the prayer diary." After much heart-searching, I decided to send it to an editor, who later recommended it to the publisher.

My motive to publish being that Christians who truly seek a deeper relationship with Jesus will be encouraged to diligently pursue God so as to hear the Holy Spirit speak deep within their hearts, where the truth will gradually become evident that Jesus is truly their personal friend, not someone remote and far-off in heaven but someone near—even within their hearts through the power of the Holy Spirit.

In this book I have revealed my struggles and triumphs. The path we walk with Jesus is not always rosy, but it can be an exciting adventure. It is not in chronological order as originally written but has been placed in chapters. Requested prayers have been deleted for privacy reasons. And some additions and changes have been made to make it more specific to the reader.

These pages take you along a journey of many years of written prayers. It contains fifty-two small chapters, one for each week of the year. Many today, in this hectic world, rush against time. You, the reader, may have quiet days within your week that allow you to read a small portion weekly along with your Bible. It is good to determine that time and keep it aside—perhaps a Sunday or whenever your schedule allows. I pray that as you read God will speak to you personally regarding your victories, strifes, and specific needs. But most importantly, I pray that you listen and hear the Holy Spirit speak within and live it out to the glory of God. Amen!

Preface

It's all about Jesus.

It's about the journey. It's seeing the heart of God.

I write to you, Lord Jesus, my deepest thoughts, feelings, aspirations, and beliefs, as I aspire to call you my friend and to share with you my innermost reflections and dreams. No appointment necessary to speak with you as to an earthly King and await his time; rather, you are here in a blink of an eye. What you did in biblical days, you do today. You speak, you care, and most of all, you love like no other. Lord Jesus, amongst the perplexities of life I hold fast to you as I endeavor to build my faith and trust you absolutely.

Father God, I'm so delighted that you are my Heavenly Father, and I can ramble on without fear that you will tire or become wearied as humans are quick to do. You take an interest in all the minuscule matters of life.

My Jesus, you are the Lord of Glory, my Monarch, the King of Kings and the Lord of Lords in addition to the Prince of Peace. You are altogether lovely; it amazes me that you care for me—that you have time for me. Dear Lord Jesus, thank you for being my friend. You are a friend above all friends, a friendship that will continue to grow with time, a friendship to treasure and value forevermore.

My Lord, I wish to renew my commitment to you that is to the furthest extent that I am able. I endeavor to humble myself under your discipline and dedicate myself entirely to you, to serve you as my King, whatever the cost may be. I pray, Jesus, that by the end of my journey through this earth life, your Holy Spirit will have fine-tuned my spirit and purified me into the incredible being you envisaged at creation. To God be the glory. Amen.

1

You Found Me

Suppose one of you has a hundred sheep and loses one of them. Does he not leave the ninety-nine in the open country and go after the lost sheep until he finds it? (Luke 15:4)

"For I know the plans I have for you," declares the Lord, "plans to prosper you and not to harm you, plans to give you hope and a future."
(Jer. 29:11)

Dear Jesus, my loving Savior, I've been deliberating upon and rejoicing about the greatest moment of my life: the day you reached down, took me under your wing, and began a work within—a work I assume will not end until I reach that beautiful and glorious place, the heavenly realm, your kingdom.

Lord, being disenchanted and disillusioned with life and the emptiness within, despondency encircled me and life was wretched and depressing, I failed to see purpose. Desperately unhappy, I repeatedly asked myself, "Is this all there is? Life is full of struggles; my marriage is crumbling. There must be something more to this earthly life." I decided to seek an answer.

As a child I was sent to Sunday school classes, and in high school I occasionally attended weekly lunchtime Bible studies—but nothing seemed to connect. Even so, Jesus, I cried out to a God who I did not know but was sure existed somewhere up there in the heavens above the stars. Somehow, I knew you had to be there. You had to be the one.

I was unsure of Christianity. Countless religions exist throughout the world. I could not believe the adage that all paths lead to heaven; it seemed self-evident that there could only be one true religion and one true God—but which one? Was it Christianity (Jesus), Buddha, Islam (Muhammad), Confucius? Can the answers be found in Judaism, or in the study of Hinduism or Shintoism? I did not know. I was resolute not to get it wrong. The deep-felt need within to find the correct path to the heavenly God enticed me to go to the library in fervent pursuit of you. I studied many of the world religions. This succeeded only in bringing upon me much confusion, and sadly I yielded to the conviction that I might never know the truth.

I was invited to attend a Protestant church where I observed all the parishioners come across as happy and content in their faith, but I spent my time tossing and turning in bed each night. I was still unsure—was this the way? I was caught in this dilemma for months.

Finally, evangelists carried out camp meetings in the area, and that was where my search ended. You found me; you reached down and touched me, dear Jesus, and showered me with a deep and inexpressible love. Peace pervaded my whole being, along with the joy of overwhelming elation, the wonder of it all, unlike anything previously experienced.

I discovered you, the creator of heaven and earth and moreover a personal friend—not someone distant, entrenched far away above the starry skies, but ever so near, even within. Jesus, you are the one!

> *My child, know that no one ever seeks me in vain. I always put myself in the way of being found; your search has not been in vain. I love you with an endearing love, a love that will by no means diminish in intensity. My love is never-ending. When events turn contrary to your wish, I will be there holding you and uplifting you—all the more so when you do not understand. Always remember this, my dear one.*

Thanks to you, Jesus, my journey has continued with you and you are dearer to me as each day goes by. You are, beyond doubt, my best friend; my heart fills with jubilation as I meditate upon you. I indeed thank you that you found me after I had given up all hope. My search is over.

Do you recall when you were in a similar situation, or when Jesus found you? Write your own prayer about it here.

Christian Growth

Be perfect, therefore, as your heavenly father is perfect.
(Matt. 5:48)

Reflect upon this verse. Is there a deep yearning to grow more like Christ?

Lord Jesus, following my initial encounter with you, the happiness that pervaded my whole being and the euphoria I felt gave way to uncertainty, as I faced the unexpected training and discipline needful for Christian growth. I yearned for transformation to grow into your likeness, but sadly I did not foresee the rocky road I had to tread.

My daughter, only I know exactly the blueprint I ordained for you from birth. It is for you to seek me and that perfect design and *to follow beside me. As you follow me closely, you will keep on the narrow road and not fall away. Satan would have you slip and unable to carry out your work, and thus delay your Christian growth. So be diligent, and do not compare yourself with others. You are unique, and the ministry I ordained for you is also unique.*

Lord Jesus, I'll endeavor not to compare myself. I thank you for lifting the habit of coveting praise and commendation from people; it cannot be found there. The secret is to continually seek after you. Jesus, by this road I endeavor to build a genuine friendship. I'm sure, Lord, that to obtain success it's imperative to keep on the narrow road and follow the plan, the roadmap you have ordained not only for me but individually for all who walk upon this earth.

Lord, you have not left us alone; you care for us and plan for us. I pray we all will follow. I believe, Jesus, that it is not realistic to anticipate perfection this side of heaven, although I'm aware to aim for less is unworthy. I pray that my witness for you is real and that the deep desire within to serve you will bear fruit. I offer my life to you to use for the realization of your ultimate plan. Jesus, I feel low today, a little pressured and incompetent.

Daughter, sometimes when my children feel at their lowest is when the most work is done for me. You have no idea, my child, how much power radiated from you today. You are one of my chosen ones, chosen for a special work. Through prayer, fasting, witnessing, and ministering, my people have a special work to do for me because I am in them guiding them. I want you to be led moment by moment by the Spirit. At other times I require you merely to sit at my feet and learn of me as did Mary of old; it's only in this way you can grow and bring other people into a deeper walk with me. So, press on, my child; each time of suffering or testing you endure brings you closer to me, and this is the training ground for this special work. Always remember that to share in my glory you must share in my sufferings. I love you so much, and someday we will spend eternity together, nevermore to be parted. There will be no more suffering there, my child.

Thank you, Jesus. No more suffering—such a joy to anticipate. Please forgive my grievances. I seek your touch, Jesus, the new life that bubbles up within, that abundant life, that life that gives peace and joy to hold forever, the most exhilarating and at the same time most peaceful experience one can obtain, the joy that no man can take away. In you, Jesus, I find a tangible sense of security.

Lord, we all strive after happiness, and many find it fleeting, for when circumstances fail to align with our wishes, happiness eludes us. This is not so with joy. Joy is everlasting, as true joy is found only in a close relationship with you. You, Jesus, are the source of all joy. Once all is surrendered to you—in whom love is unconditional and everlasting—this joy is ours.

Jesus, my misdemeanors, frustrations, and misunderstandings disturb me. I hand these over to you, and ask for aid to overcome every mountain of difficulty in my life. My priority is to develop my Christian walk, to grow in faith, and to become one with you. Hallelujah, how great would that be! To assist this, time spent with you is of the essence, to seek a close affinity with you. Thus, you must work first within before you work through us.

The Bible says that the fear of God is the beginning of wisdom. I believe, Jesus, that wisdom is vital—to humble ourselves and give thanks to you for the peace that passes all understanding and for the faith that moves mountains, to seek wisdom in all our decisions is paramount; this, I presume, is your wish. Your Word promises, "According to your faith will it be done to you" (Matt. 9:29). I pray, most of all, that pride be destroyed within. I love you, Lord. I love the "love chapter," where I am encouraged to grow my faith and understand that love never fails (1 Cor. 13), and I know it's true—you never fail, as God is love.

I sorely fail, Lord. I need your guidance, to hear your voice more distinctly and to distinguish your will unmistakably. It does take perseverance to sacrifice our time, to be still in your presence, and to listen quietly. These exercises revitalize our souls and bodies. Lord Jesus, the task is not straightforward as we race to keep up with our heavy schedules in this frenzied world. The wheels ought to be slowed.

This morning, Jesus, I read where Paul said, "Keep your roots deep in him, build your lives on him, and become stronger in your faith, as you were taught" (Col. 2:7, GNT). At once a vision appeared: a plant cutting in a glass of water. I saw tiny roots appearing, and instantly knew it was symbolic of me and my Christian growth. My roots had indeed begun to grow, but I was stunned to notice how tiny, weak, and thin they were. O my Lord, they must grow and become more robust, or else (the plant) my spirit will wither and my desire for you wane. Truly, my Lord, it's so necessary that your support is ensured. Jesus, please intercede on my behalf so that my heart will wax warmer and knowledge of you will grow greater.

We pray this in order that you may live a life worthy of the Lord . . . growing in the knowledge of God. (Col. 1:10)

What are some of the difficulties you encounter in your desire to build your Christian growth?

Whittling

I am the true vine, and my Father is the gardener. He cuts off every branch in me that bears no fruit, while every branch that does bear fruit he prunes so that it will be even more fruitful.
(*John 15:1–2*)

The whittling, pruning, and molding is not always easy, don't you agree?

I encourage you to take time to applaud God for his work within your life.

What a glorious morning, Jesus! I read in *Come Away My Beloved* where you said, "I wait for you to turn from everything else to me alone. I want the real you. The more you can bring to me of your true self, the more I can give to you of my true self."[1]

Jesus, this is such an admirable goal. How important it is to reveal our hearts and be real. Honesty is of primary importance—to be honest with you, with others, and with ourselves. Lord, the truth is it is often difficult to be honest with ourselves. It's difficult to see ourselves as others see us or as you see us, to see what needs changing, shaping, or whittling.

You, my Lord, wish all Christians to be lights shining in the world, to declare your love by our love and witness. I pray that will bring joy to your heart. We all must wait on you, although waiting is one of the hardest and most tedious things to do. Waiting on you, I realize, is not to sit and fantasize but requires harnessing our thoughts. This is another facet of waiting: it takes effort to totally center our minds on you and to enable your love to flood over us and within us. The scripture says, "Blessed are all who wait for him!" (Isa. 30:18).

I'm aware, Jesus, that for me there's a further need for whittling to achieve this. The whittling necessary for Christian growth can be quite unpleasant and even detestable at times; likewise, I'm mindful that some readers may find this to be their experience, too. Even so, it brings forth the beautiful ordained image you had in mind as you created us. King David said in Psalms: "You created my inmost being; you knit me together in my mother's womb. I praise you because I am fearfully and wonderfully made" (Ps. 139:13–14).

In life, Jesus, I see you use struggle, failure, and discouragement to whittle away unnecessary preoccupations that are not of you and to mold and fashion us in your image. This may not have been appreciated at the time! In retrospect, though, these times of difficulty and whittling have enabled a measure of patience, perseverance, and obedience. Our glorious Lord, you desire only the highest good for your children. You are so patient. It is true you created us to worship and glorify you. Lord, I request the magnificent fruit of the Spirit so we may all add to our faith and exhibit "love, joy, peace, patience, kindness, goodness, faithfulness, gentleness and self-control" (Gal. 5:22–23). I pray also for the gifts of the Spirit to be manifested within our ministries, which your Holy Spirit gives to each as he wills. I pray for Christians, especially those who are seeking a closer walk and deeper bond with you, Lord Jesus—that they will come through the whittling period renewed and purified.

In *God Calling*, I read: "What if the pipe were to say, 'I do so little, I wish I could be more use.' The reply would be 'It is not you, but the water that passes through you, that saves and blesses. All you have to do is to see there is nothing to block the way so that the water cannot flow through.'"[2]

Jesus, I imagine the water symbolizes the Holy Spirit; the pipe, the hose, represents the flesh. It's crucial not to obstruct the Spirit's work but to allow it to flow freely. As self is crucified, the Holy Spirit is given free rein to work miraculously within, to whittle away much that is ungodly, and to shape all that is godly. It is vital to cling tightly to you and direct our focus more upon you than upon self. Self is the real problem.

Consider therefore the kindness and sternness of God: sternness to those who fell, but kindness to you, provided that you continue in his kindness. Otherwise, you also will be cut off.
(Rom. 11:22)

What is your response to the whittling within your own life? Write your thoughts below.

Clinging to You

When he came, and had seen the grace of God, was glad, and exhorted them all, that with purpose of heart they would cleave unto the Lord.
(Acts 11:23, KJV)

I am always with you; you hold me by my right hand . . . it is good to be near God
(Ps. 73:23, 28)

Jesus desires all to cling to him, cleave to him, be near to him, and hold tightly to him.

My prayer is that all who read this book would do so.

Dear Jesus, you promised you will always be with us. Sometimes it seems that you are far away; nevertheless, deep within, I'm aware it is *I* who am far away. In spite of this, Jesus, I cling to you in desperation.

You do well to cling, as I am the refuge you desire and need. I am your all. I go before you to prepare the way; I smooth the path and clear away the briars before you. Seek me, and you will find. Do not do as many do—go their own way to their own detriment. I have said I will never leave nor forsake you. Always remember that. It applies to all my children as well as to you, my dear child.

I do remember, Lord. I remember too, your method of teaching. You use all our circumstances to teach lessons. Nothing you allow in our lives is wasted. After becoming a Christian, I attended a mainstream church; as you were aware, I was quite ignorant of the Scriptures but had an intense appetite for the Word of God. I was elated when a couple of ladies asked permission to study the Bible with me. I enjoyed the instruction with these lovely ladies and looked forward to their visit each week. However, with more knowledge of the Bible, confusion set in.

Thankfully, Jesus, a verse in Acts spoke of Paul preaching in the synagogue in Berea: "[The Bereans] examined the Scriptures every day to see if what Paul said was true" (Acts 17:11).

I purchased a concordance, took note of the Bereans, and continued to check. What I was taught every so often did not align with the Bible or the pastor's sermons; it was all so perplexing.

Later an invitation arrived inviting me to become a member of their church, which was declined. The following day, on answering the doorbell, the two ladies stood there and in between them for an instant I saw a wolf—a man who came to convince me to attend their place of worship. I'm grateful to you, Jesus, for giving me spiritual insight and revealing the wolf. A verse I had previously read in Acts came to mind: "I know that after I leave, savage wolves will come among you and will not spare the flock" (Acts 20:29). The timing of your warning was exemplary. I needed to be aware, heed you, and cling closely to you, Jesus, so to not be enticed away. Thanks to you, Lord, I'm now in a new church where I attend Bible study with amazing Christians. But it is you, Holy Spirit, who is the perfect teacher.

The need for all Christians to cling closely to you is vital—to embrace you and receive that invigorating life that flows from you, renewing our fainting spirit and reviving our strength—to "seek first his kingdom and his righteousness" (Matt. 6:33). This is my wish: to cling to you and become more like you in righteousness.

Our greatest blessing is to come near you to sit at your feet, like Mary. Her sister Martha, who complained of Mary's choice, had the idea that serving you was best. I'm certain other people may have thought the same. Serving you is great—but desiring you, loving you, learning from you, sitting in your presence simply clinging to you and growing into your likeness is of far greater worth. To *be* is better than to *do*. Doing will flow out of being. It's love that's the greatest. Jesus, I can see King Solomon's great love shown in this verse: "[S]how me your face, let me hear your voice; for your voice is sweet, and your face is lovely" (Song 2:14).

When you have had an over-the-moon experience of God's love—or, on the other hand, felt that life's struggles were just too much and all you craved was just to cling to Him?

It is good to write your feelings down in prayer.

_____
_____
_____
_____
_____
_____
_____
_____
_____
_____
_____
_____
_____
_____
_____
_____
_____
_____
_____

All Things Work Together for Good

And we know that in all things God works for the good of those who love him, who have been called according to his purpose. For those God foreknew he also predestined to be conformed to the likeness of his Son.
(Rom. 8:28–29)

Meditate for a moment on what these verses say to you.

Jesus, I sense these verses signify that you are building holiness of character into our lives, so that we may be conformed to your likeness. "All things" means not only the good but the grave as well, right? You are constantly occupied on your created masterpieces, to bring greatness into our lives. There is no greater goal than to grow

Christlike—to seek your help first, to hand over every moment of each day to you, to expect nothing of the world and know nothing but you, Lord Jesus. As our focus is continually upon you, our lives are revitalized and our souls invigorated. Glorious Lord, the way to your heart is to constantly praise and thank you for all things, and to be so fine-tuned to you that we shall speak heart to heart instead of mind to mind.

Jesus, it is trials that strengthen our spiritual muscles and transport us into your desired place. Your ways are different from ours; you bring love, joy, peace, and security into our lives, but you might also step aside and allow whatever Satan brings upon us. You likewise close the door on Satan if it does not accomplish your purpose. As I place my life in your hands, I see all as coming from you.

Jesus, we live in a fallen world with dire economic problems and cruel terror attacks, as well as harsh personal trials; and at times it appears you have withdrawn and evil forces have triumphed. However, it is true that we ought not fear, as you are still in control. Job was faithful to you, and eventually all worked out in his favor; in fact, he was doubly blessed. You are the same yesterday and today and forever (Heb. 13:8). We too can experience the blessings of Job. Jesus, it is true; Christians are on the winning side!

It is true that you fight for us. "[T]he LORD your God is the one who goes with you to fight for you against your enemies to give you victory" (Deut. 20:4). Lord, our enemies may not only be the evil spirits or the people who wish to torment us but the enemies within, those unworthy preoccupations that steal our time and lead us nowhere. We all need to overcome these as we take the road of adventure with you.

Jesus, I appreciate that you work for our good, even to fight against our enemies. That is great news. Our greatest enemy, Satan, tempts, beguiles, and deceives. One tactic he has up his sleeve is to interrupt our prayer life. Prayer and praise repulse him. The devil is surely an entity of pretense and the father of lies! He deceives unbelievers—some into believing he does not exist, and others into believing that he is God himself. It is your Spirit, Jesus, who enables us to overcome the temptations of Satan. I thank you, glorious Savior, that you work out all our failures for our good. But I do still seek your approval and forgiveness.

My child, you have my approval, and your sins are forgiven. So, go now, walk in humility and joy, and show the world the love and joy you gain from communion with me, your beloved Savior, Lord, and King.

To seek God in the early morning is to emulate both Jesus and King David, who sought God early. Do you seek him early?

Pray about this and see God work all things out for your good.

Glorious Savior

Dear friends, now we are children of God, and what we will be has not yet been known. But we know that when he appears, we shall be like him, for we shall see him as he is. Everyone who has this hope in him purifies himself, just as he is pure.
(1 John 3:2–3)

Visualize the change when we view our new purified spiritual bodies in heaven.
How glorious!

What a lovely morning, Jesus. You are rightly our glorious Savior, our majestic God! This is a new day, and I will glory in you and rejoice. I know that a joyful and abundant life is possible with your blessing. As we all walk in obedience and follow your instructions, that abundant life will be ours.

Jesus, it's just superb to relax in the sunshine by the beach and marvel at your creativity. Your creation is beyond words. To hear the gentle sound of the flowing surf, and recall the furious pounding of waves against the cliffs. The potential energy of the ocean that can capsize the greatest of ships shows your mighty, dramatic power and creativity.

When I reflect upon you, Jesus, and see you as our glorious Savior, I repent. I wish to ask your forgiveness, sweet Jesus, for the many times spent blaming you for not coming to my rescue. Recognition of this attitude is simply passivity; my aspiration for you was to simply zap me and turn me into some kind of "Wonder Woman." I wished for the abundant life without the effort, discipline, and trials needed to bring me to that point. James says, "Faith without deeds is dead" (Jas. 2:26). I'm aware of what to do, but passivity is the problem. Jesus, truly my objective is to be like you. To grow into your likeness is the highest goal. None other is worthy to emulate, only you, Jesus, our magnificent Savior.

Today I read the Scripture that says that you were not housed in a body so beautiful: "He had no beauty or majesty to attract us to him, nothing in his appearance that we should desire him" (Isa. 53:2). Lord Jesus, even as the Scripture said, on earth you had no beauty to attract us, but without doubt your spirit and character are lovely. Even if you were the ugliest person on the planet, I would still love you and long to be with you and chat with you. You are the kindest, humblest, most loving, and most compassionate person in the entire universe. It is true that your dealings and actions in our lives are all performed in love. You could not do otherwise, as you are God and God is love. Jesus, truly you are the Glorious One.

My sweet dear child—how sweet you are, the apple of my eye. Your longing to be as I am will be answered in a way you know not. You will be changed from glory to glory. Do not keep questioning, only trust; I am your loving God, also your faithful friend. Please allow me to be all that you require. I fill the gaps in your life; I lift the burdens you carry, so you may walk into the sunlit glades with light and joyful steps to welcome me, and in me you will have your needs met. Believe me, my child, and love me as I love you.

Jesus, my heart leaps for joy! Lord, I do love you. I scarcely believe that I am worthy of such attention. Actually, no one is worthy; it's by grace that your love is gifted, poured out upon us. You are so gracious. You are not a man that you should lie, as in Scripture it is written, "I am the way and the *truth* and the life" (John 14:6, emphasis added). Jesus, whatever you say is gospel. You have richly blessed me through your words. I pray I may learn to trust your Word—even the *rhema,* your spoken word, when applied to me. In fact, Lord, this applies to all your children.

It is true, Lord, that you are the one through whom all blessings flow. Great joy and contentment in heart and mind come from knowing who we are in Christ. Your extravagant and unwarranted love is astonishing. Jesus, your eternal love makes me worship in awe; you are our incredible Savior. We need not fear death. Knowing our eternal destiny where sin dwells no more, death has no dread for us; we will reside with you for eternity.

How great is the love the Father has lavished on us, that we should be called children of God! (1 John 3:1)

This is how God showed his love among us: He sent his one and only Son into the world that we might live through him. (1 John 4:9)

Which characteristics of your glorious Savior would you wish to model yourself?

Sin

Everyone who sins breaks the law; in fact, sin is lawlessness. But you know that he appeared so that he might take away our sins. (1 John 3:4–5)

For Christ died for sins once for all, the righteous for the unrighteous, to bring you to God. (1 Pet. 3:18)

What effect does sin have on our relationship with God? Pray and ask forgiveness for any unconfessed sin within your own life.

There is one who is totally without sin, pure and holy—and that one is you, Jesus. Your disciple John said of you, "And in him is no sin. No one who lives in him keeps on sinning. No one who continues to sin has either seen him or known him" (1 John 3:5–6). In your Word are instructions for Christian growth. But iniquity within our lives delays this growth.

Your Word makes it clear that those ferocious, degraded depravities of murder, adultery, rape, assault, terrorism, homosexuality, pride, and theft are not the only iniquities that war against our souls—there's also doubt, fear, selfishness, self-centeredness, self-indulgence, self-pity, temper, impatience, criticism, and worry. It's easy to condone these latter transgressions, but sin is sin!

Even the smallest sin does not go unobserved by you, Lord, does it? Words hurt, Jesus; it may not always be the actual words spoken but the tone used. Words are powerful. It's the words we voice and the way we voice them that can make the difference, whether they wound or uplift. Jesus, you see our hearts and motives; what we say must be said in love or it is sin. You say that we must account for every careless word spoken.

Jesus, I pray as did King David, "Turn to me and be gracious to me, for I am lonely and afflicted. The troubles of my heart have multiplied; free me from my anguish. Look upon my affliction and see my distress and take away all my sins" (Ps. 25:16–18).

Various ones of this world reject you, Jesus; they do their own thing, go their own way, and do it to their own detriment. The love displayed at Calvary, Jesus, was not only for your nearest and dearest friends or only for "good" people but also for your enemies; you love all equally. But scores choose to harden their hearts and ears against the Holy Spirit in disbelief and slowly become deafened to his voice. The

Spirit then beckons them no longer. This, I dare say, Jesus, is the unforgivable sin.

Before you came into our lives, sin had us in its clutches. Even long after conversion, Jesus, I justified myself; I found it hard to overcome those sins that I considered minor. But there is no defense. The Holy Spirit within gives us the power and enables us to rebuke the temptation of the evil one and to rise to victory. I am without excuse! I repent of my offences, such as doubt and worry. Sin is a separating agent and is repulsive to you, especially the evils of self-centeredness and self-pity as these offences can prevent the divine life, that outpouring joy, from flowing through us.

Lord, when joy is absent and your voice silent, my query is this: Is this the result of disobedience to your instructions or perhaps deafness to your voice?

My child, sin is forgiven when you repented. But dear one, do you not know there are often consequences to sin?

Thanks be to you, Lord Jesus. You died in our place and connected all the faithful to the Father through the cross—the cross on which you died, the cross on which our sins were nailed. You defeated death, and through your resurrection, we who put our trust in you live. Praise to you, most Holy One, for the sacrifice made for all mankind. I thank you for your forgiveness and pray I may not commit the same iniquities again. I'm sorry for my transgressions and my neglect of you.

I seek forgiveness for worry. Where does worry get us? Nowhere. I've been a worrywart. Worry shows a lack of trust, a total lack of faith in you. I pray I may untangle the web I've wrapped around myself by anxiety. Lord Jesus, why should any be anxious? It is nonsensical, especially as you are here to lead and guide us along that exclusive path, that path divinely mapped out. I ask forgiveness for my self-doubt. There is still too much of me, myself, and I. I confess I'm guilty; but you, Lord, are perfect.

Jesus, your plans for your children are eternally for our benefit. Though we may give into temptation and transgress, or drift away, no enemy can thwart your final plan. Thank you that you are habitually working to draw us back to you. I thank you, Lord, for your great love and clemency for all Christians who may struggle in various areas. Please help us repent and humble ourselves under your discipline. We are new creations, but still sin—perhaps not in ghastly ways, but there is no trivial sin.

Love does cover a multitude of sins—sins that have been confessed and washed by your blood. My Lord, I pray for myself and for other Christians who sometimes struggle, much as King David did in the Psalms: "Hide your face from my sins and blot out all my iniquity. Create in me a pure heart, O God, and renew a steadfast spirit within me" (Ps. 51:9–10); "Forgive my hidden faults. . . . Then will I be blameless, innocent of great transgression. May the words of my mouth and the meditation of my heart be pleasing in your sight, O LORD, my Rock and my Redeemer" (Ps. 19:12–14). We have no need to worry, as our conscience is cleansed through the blood of the Lamb who purifies us.

Jesus, I give thanks to you who lifted us out of this sordid world with its enticements and distractions and into your amazing grace. This is the marvel of Calvary. My confidence is in you, Jesus.

He who does what is sinful is of the devil, because the devil has been sinning from the beginning. The reason the Son of God appeared was to destroy the devil's work.
(1 John 3:8)

Is it problematic to envisage an invisible God and devil? How do you see these two who are total opposites? Take time to confess your misdemeanors in prayer to your Heavenly Father in the name of Jesus. Write down your praises to Jesus for his sacrifice and for his forgiveness of sins.

_____
_____
_____
_____
_____
_____
_____
_____
_____
_____
_____
_____
_____
_____
_____
_____
_____
_____
_____
_____

Your Love

Who, then, can separate us from the love of Christ?
(Rom. 8:35, GNT)

This is how we know what love is: Jesus Christ laid down his life for us. (1 John 3:10)

Do you recall when these verses first touched your life? Ponder God's love for you.

Dear Jesus, your love is the most formidable, the most powerful force in the universe. Actually, it is what one would call indefinable love—so it is to mere mortals. You are superior to any picture, theory, or notion we could possibly envision in our minds. I applaud you, Lord Jesus, and praise you for your love, joy, and peace, although their depths are unfathomable. Submerged deeper than all human knowledge. In quiet times, coupled together with all who come to you in the quietness of their prayer closets, there you speak deep secrets and hidden truths into our hearts, where we gain a small glimpse of your most endearing love.

First Thessalonians says, "Be joyful always; pray continually; give thanks in all circumstances, for this is God's will for you in Christ Jesus" (1 Thess. 5:16–18). I implore you, Lord, fill me with joy and give me a great love for you. I pray especially that you would help me in your search for lost souls, and in addition give me faith and boldness in speaking your Word, so that unbelievers will believe. Jesus, I pray also for my family.

> *My hand is heavily upon your family. My Holy Spirit is striving with each one, and I will be victorious in their lives. As you know, my child, I love all my children and want the best for each and every one.*

The Bible says, "God is love" (1 John 4:8, 16). The intensity of your love, Jesus, was revealed on the cross when you died for the sins of mankind. You took our sin upon yourself and endured the punishment due us so we might be forgiven and saved. It is essential to gaze upon the cross, to see the scale of your love. I pray that because of your sacrifice many eyes and hearts will open to you, Jesus—to see you as their Savior, accept you as their Redeemer and Lord, and be cleansed from all immorality and wrongdoing.

It astounds me; death could not hold you. You rose victoriously from the grave, giving those who believe victory over eternal death. Your resurrection was our salvation, our redemption; we can now enjoy all it encompasses. Indeed, your love does conquer all. I thank you and praise you, Jesus, that you died that we might live. Once we have a vision of your generous and undeserved love, who could fail to declare faith in you and love you in return?

Lord Jesus, as we continue to place our trust in you, I pray that your will for our lives will be made plain and that our love for you will continue to significantly increase. Shine your light brightly upon us. I await with anticipation a revival to spread forth throughout our country.

Thank you also, Holy Father, for the Holy Spirit revival we are already seeing, especially in the Third World, as well as undercover in the Middle East. In my country, numerous people are affluent and worldly without a care. I'm saddened for them as they know not the times we are living in or what they forego. They fail to experience your love that is far beyond human words to express. This world that so entices offers nothing but the abyss. I implore you, Jesus, for revival within our hearts. Thank you for your promise to all humanity.

> *My love is so great for all my created ones—even those whose sins have not been repented of, even those who will eventually go into the abyss. No matter the wickedness, no matter the depravity of their lives, if they would truly repent and ask forgiveness with a broken and contrite heart and come to me, I would save them.*

Our glorious Redeemer, it is impossible to estimate the measure of your magnificence and the magnitude of your redeeming love—that powerful love that allows us to see beyond hurts and offenses to your saving grace.

God is love. (1 John 4:8, 16)

*[Nothing] will be able to separate us from the love of God that is in Christ Jesus our Lord.
(Rom. 8:39)*

Love is power, the greatest power on earth. Pen your thoughts below on these powerful verses.

Overcoming Temptation

Be self-controlled and alert. Your enemy the devil prowls around like a roaring lion looking for someone to devour.
(1 Pet. 5:8)

How often are you shocked when an ugly
thought enters your mind?
Consider this: Could it have been planted by
the evil one?

Lord Jesus, it's troubling that billions reject your most endearing love, that intensifying love showered down upon us. We are all so sinful! When you, Jesus, created this world, it was "good." In fact, when you created mankind, it was "very good." But now, because of the evil one's temptation, the earth is a den of thieves through greed and lust for power. These cause most of our woes worldwide. Our problems are not always due to policy; we have a heart problem. Changing laws or dropping bombs will not change the hatred that is imbedded within. You only, Lord, have the ability to change the human heart, reveal sin and pride, and empower us to overcome the temptation to sin. But you will not violate our free will.

Jesus, as I awoke this morning, I saw a skinny yellowish-green snake pop its head out from under my sleeve, revealing its fangs. My interpretation of this vision: The snake represents Satan, the serpent. As its fangs were out, it was ready to strike. Lord, there is such a need to constantly be aware of the evil one's temptations and to keep close to you, as our place of safety is in your presence. Satan endeavors to tempt us into wickedness, but the Holy Spirit enables us to stand our ground. I do so appreciate your guidance. I fear, Lord, that the evil one's strike cannot always be evaded, no matter who it comes through. However, with your power, I can stand and not be moved. Thank you for your warning.

Lord, there are numbers of pastors who often fail their congregations by neglecting to preach or warn against Satan's temptations and his demonic activities—I presume from fear of upsetting or alarming their parishioners or fear they may depart, leaving the coffers empty. It's worrying, Jesus, as being silent allows the devil free rein to trap, deceive, and fool their congregations unaware; as a consequence, they are left ill equipped to stand against him. Lord, I sense that in this present age, Satan's temptations will increase as we near the predicted tribulation. Your wish for us is not to be focused on evil but to be continually focused on you. But we are to be aware!

Father, I ask why did you not kick Lucifer, the devil, out of the universe when he first turned against you? O forgive me, Heavenly Father, that I should question you—I do appreciate that there is a perfect reason and purpose for all you do, and eternally your purpose is and always will be for the betterment of mankind.

I pray to you, Father God, in the greatest name amongst those in heaven and on earth: the name of Jesus Christ. Lord, help me; I despair of my failure. I feel like Paul when he said, "I do not understand what I do. For what I want to do I do not do, but what I hate I do" (Rom. 7:15). My prayer, Lord, is that you support me and empower my children who are struggling against temptation. May we all overcome and conquer in your strength.

I pray to be true to the vision envisaged when you created me. To be separated from the world, as in this world there is selfishness and greed, a "what's in it for me?" mentality. You also wish us to avoid pride, that selfsame sin Satan committed. In your world is humility, loving, and giving. I envision heaven as beyond description, too splendid for words. No temptation. Jesus, you have given a number of people visions of heaven, and some have been taken up for a visit. Had I been on a visit, I would loathe to be sent back, after partaking of the beauties and splendors of paradise.

It's tremendous that you made a way where there was no way. The cross was the answer to our struggle with the sinful nature. Words fail to praise you adequately for taking our sin and our punishment upon yourself. You freed us to enter heaven when we believed, repented, relied on, and trusted in you. All glory to you, Lord Jesus, for our salvation and the power you give that enables us to overcome temptation.

My child, look always to me, putting out temptation immediately as you have been doing. Try to know the difference between what is temptation and what is sin; then you won't despair so much over times you think you have sinned but have not. This is a trick of the evil one, to burden you with false sin. Today is perfect; enjoy the sunshine. I send it for your enjoyment.

Jesus, at times Satan blinds us to sin. I'm sure it's one of his tricks, as he is the deceiver and tempter of mankind. Sin can appear pleasurable, and thus gives him easy access into people's lives. We need to fight temptation like the plague, don't we, Lord?

Watch and pray so that you will not fall into temptation. The spirit is willing, but the body is weak.
(Matt. 26:41)

Respond to this verse. This may well be a chance to pray about any sin or temptation within your own life, and to write your thanks to Jesus for forgiveness.

The Time for Salvation

For it is by grace you have been saved, through faith—and this is not from yourselves, it is a gift from God.
(Eph. 2:8)

Dwell upon the wonderful day you were saved, and give all praise to Jesus.

Jesus, it is beyond reason why certain people turn away from a free gift—especially the gift of salvation, as you are so ready to pardon. It's difficult to understand and so sad.

Child, the time has come for all to repent of their evil, lustful ways and to look to the God who is supreme and almighty, who can save *them out of the troubles which they have brought upon themselves.*

Lord Jesus, as a new day begins, I repent of my transgressions. I put my life into your hands to lead, guide, and direct me. I ask your help to overcome all that is within and all that comes against me. I put on the whole armor of God: the belt of truth, the breastplate of righteousness, and the shoes of peace. I take up the shield of faith and put on the helmet of salvation and the sword of the Spirit to stand against the wiles of Satan and his demons (Eph. 6:13–17). I claim your blood over me, your blood that was shed at Calvary to wash, cleanse, and purify all imperfections within. I give thanks to you, Lord, that you protect and perfect and heal.

Praise you, Lord, for this special training, and the blueprint designed before birth; with your assistance, Jesus, I'll endeavor to follow it diligently. I pray, Jesus, that you will empower us to become missionaries in our own homes, in our neighborhoods, or wherever you place us, so that we together may shine your light and light up this dark world. I pray that numerous folk will glance up, see your radiant light, and come to you for salvation.

Dear Jesus, I'm troubled for the people around me. Please empower those who know you, and fast-track those who do not. Billions are ignorant of the times we are living in; many, with no dread of hell, walk the way of turmoil and gnashing of teeth without any fear or anguish at all. Whenever the word "hell" comes up, degenerate men laugh and reply that they'll have lots of mates down there; while women invariably say they will go to heaven, as they are good and have never hurt anyone. These ideas are deceptive and give people a false sense of security.

These men are deceived; there is no love in hell—the impression I get is they'll hate each other, mates no longer! Jesus, "good" has nothing to do with it. Their righteousness is not sufficient to earn their own salvation. It's what you accomplished on the cross; it's our faith in you and this accomplishment that gives us redemption. Isn't that so, Jesus?

> *I did not say if you are good you will go to heaven; that's the lie of Satan. My Word said that whoever believes in me shall not perish but have eternal life. (John 3:16)*

Not all "good works" are blessed by you, God—only the works the Holy Spirit performs through his surrendered vessels. Help me, Lord, to differentiate between good and God.

Jesus, I know countless lovely, polite, courteous people who would not dare utter a hurtful word, but it breaks my heart if they do not come to know you as Lord and Savior before the judgment; at that point, salvation is lost, and their destination is the abyss. O Jesus, this is too horrendous to contemplate. I pray, Lord, for many to read and see you in Scripture; the Bible is the most powerful book in the world. I sincerely pray that eyes and hearts will open to the reality that it is time for salvation, and that they will look up and view you in all your glory and consequently reach out to you and be saved. Now is the day of salvation!

I fear for those who do not know you. I pray they will not end in the devil's domain! You said, "Call to me and I will answer you and tell you great and unsearchable things you do not know" (Jer. 33:3). You, God, know the thoughts of men and search their hearts. As we call to you, Lord, in sincerity—no matter what life we have lived, whether one of indifference or of the most debased sin ever committed—you will forgive, and salvation will be attained. Jesus, numerous people appear to have little comprehension of sin. Are we, as parents, responsible for that?

> My Word states, "Train a child in the way he should go, and when he is old he will not turn from it" (Prov. 22:6). Parents are not doing that today.

This answer troubles me for my own children. I came to know you after my youngest daughter's birth. My older children suffered much from confusion due to differences in belief between their father and me. In the depths of my heart I pray they will turn with all their being to you, Jesus, and find redemption through the straight and narrow path which leads to you and to salvation, to deliverance.

I tell you, now is the time of God's favor, now is the day of salvation. (1 Cor. 6:2)

Are there lost souls among the people you love? Write a prayer below right now, for them to ultimately come into glory.

11

Transparency

Have you ever attempted to hide anything from the all-knowing God?

Child, I know you inside out. It is not possible to hide anything from me. I long for you to be transparent with me and with others.

Jesus, I don't understand. I thought I *was* transparent. I confess each sin as I become aware of it, and I even ask forgiveness for any unidentified sins I may have committed in ignorance. Heavenly Father, I come again to you in Jesus' name and confess my transgressions committed unknowingly. I guess there are many unknown sins, sins I'm unaware of. I pray they will be revealed in your good time so that I may confess and overcome them—and be saved from committing them again and again!

You, Jesus, value transparency; it's foolishness to conceal anything from you. You are the all-seeing God. There is nothing you don't know, nothing you cannot do. You surely are the all-powerful and loving God.

Remember, my child, what I said about transparency.

Lord, you know everything—what are you talking about? I know, I know that you want me to type my transgression into this book.

Child, I do not wish for you to carry pride in your heart. You must be transparent. I want you to be a radiant light to show the way to me. If you, child, have covered and hidden sin, don't you know it will eventually be brought to light?

Why, Lord? All right, I will type and confess it here, as you have asked.

Here is the truth: Before I became Christian, before I came to know you, my boyfriend and I committed fornication. Then, my boyfriend wasn't ready for marriage but we wed anyway. It was a financial struggle at first, but as time progressed and with promotions, we were financially secure. Still, it was an unhappy union almost from the start. I lived in domestic violence. Perhaps I was as much to blame as he was, Jesus. He felt trapped;

he was a free spirit, and resented being tied down in marriage. Unfortunately, he blamed me.

My mind was forever on suicide; it consumed me. I bought sleeping tablets to save up; I wanted out of this world. But I was ignorant as to how many I needed; I didn't wish to remain in a vegetable state. Jesus, all I wanted was love; I felt unlovable. My self-esteem, at that time, was at its lowest point. I imagined the children would fare better without me; I realize now that was a lie of Satan. Jesus, I was floundering in a dark world of my own, and I wanted out.

I unburdened my heart to my doctor, an orthopaedic surgeon I had been seeing for treatment. He wrapped his arms around me, and this was the start of our relationship. I then thought life wasn't at all that bad—only this relationship ended in pregnancy. I poured the sleeping tablets down the sink, as I needed to protect my unborn babe.

Today I'm a Christian, and I am overwhelmed with love for you and overwhelmed with the intensity of your love for me, Jesus. Because I love you, I try always to please you. I sense such great guilt and find it hard to forgive myself. Had I only known you earlier, my thoughts and actions would have taken a 180-degree turn—as they did when first I met you.

Jesus, why did you encourage me to type this out? Why bring it to light? It was blocked out. I would have preferred to have left it in the dark recesses of my mind.

Lord, I now confess this sin to you and ask for forgiveness. My aim is to demonstrate transparency with you and with others. I appreciate that my sin has been nailed to the cross. Today the slate is clean. I am spotless before you, if not to others. Thanks to you, Jesus, because of your sacrifice I am forgiven, sanctified, and purified. Jesus, I wish to tell others that your forgiveness is a cleansing and purifying agent. When you, Jesus, set us free, we are free indeed and victory is certain. I thank you and give all honor to you, my Lord and Savior.

Flee from sexual immorality. All other sins a man commits are outside his body, but he who sins sexually sins against his own body. Do you not know that your body is a temple of the Holy Spirit, who is in you, whom you have received from God? You are not your own; you were bought at a price. Therefore, honor God with your body.
(1 Cor. 6:18–20)

What are Jesus' commands for Christians, according to these verses? Jot them down here; they are important.

Victor

*The sting of death is sin, and the power of sin is the law.
But thanks be to God! He gives us the victory through
our Lord Jesus Christ.
(1 Cor. 15:56–57)*

Contemplate the light gained from this verse.
What is God saying here?

The sins of my past distress me—but you rescued me. Jesus, we all deserve your wrath and condemnation. However, you are the God who loves all. You are our great High Priest who intercedes for us, redeems us, frees us from sin and death, and gives us victory. Our spiritual growth is hindered if sin still has its hold on us. In view of this, I repent of the iniquities I see in my life today. Jesus, you as Victor can change me from self-centeredness to Christ-centeredness. Lord, this I wrestle with; this I fail to do alone. Please help me sacrifice all that is ungodly within. I cling to this verse: "Therefore, if anyone is in Christ, he is a new creation; the old is gone, the new has come!" (2 Cor. 5:17). Sin need not hold power over any who repents and confesses. In this we may always rejoice, that your victory, dear Jesus, enables our victory.

I thank you that you defeated Satan when you rose again. His head is now crushed, as predicted in Genesis 3:15. Clearly, Jesus, you are the Victor. Satan now has no power over us but through our own deliberate choices. On occasions when I give into temptation, I sense I've failed you. It is abhorrent to oppose you, my Lord, and a terrible injustice to you. But thank you, Jesus, that nothing can separate us from your love.

Jesus, you voluntarily died for our transgressions. I feel remorseful even to write about it, as it's difficult to imagine the extent of your suffering. I'm saddened to think that you were tempted more than any other, as I imagine the powers of hell stretched to their utmost came against you with all their might in their frenzied attempt to break you.

Speaking of you in Scripture, Isaiah wrote, "his appearance was so disfigured beyond that of any man and his form marred beyond human likeness" (Isa. 52:14). Lord, these words are difficult to digest. It makes me weep as I think of the excruciating pain of the cross; it's unthinkable—and prior to this was the terrible whipping; physically you were marred beyond recognition. In addition, Jesus, I envisage the emotional aspect: your friends the disciples' desertion, the grief of rejection and isolation, the leaders' jealousy, the spitting, the agony of separation from your Father. This was the cost you were willing to pay because of your love for everyone who lives on this planet, your created Ones.

None can imagine the degree of your suffering. To me, Jesus, the vision of Isaiah is unimaginable; it crushes my heart. But no matter the efforts made to conquer you; they could not succeed. You are invincible. You conquered them. Had you not sacrificed yourself and overcome death and Satan, we all would have been doomed.

I wish to show my gratitude by endeavoring not to give the deceiver even one conquest over my life. Lord, I am aware that total success will not be obtained this side of heaven—the closer I come to you, the more I develop an awareness of my own frailty and vulnerability. Nevertheless, you were victorious, and defeated death and gained victory for all who repent and seek forgiveness.

[F]or everyone born of God overcomes the world.
This is the victory that has overcome the world, even our faith.
Who is it that overcomes the world? Only he who believes that
Jesus is the Son of God.
(1 John 5:4–5)

Delight in Jesus—that in this truth, we too can gain victory as we hold fast to the Victor.

Forgiveness

If you forgive men when they sin against you, your heavenly Father will also forgive you. But if you do not forgive men their sins, your Father will not forgive your sins.
(Matt. 6:14–15)

But I tell you who hear me: Love your enemies, do good to those who hate you, bless those who curse you, pray for those who mistreat you. (Luke 6:27–28)

Reflect upon these verses. What can you take away from them for your own personal growth?

Dear Jesus, the costly gift of forgiveness for our sin came at the price of your life. Forgiveness is such an essential aspect of our Christian walk. If we all could forgive as you forgive, how glorious would our lives be?

> *My dear child, you know what is needed to live the victorious life, but that must be your life experience. Simply obey my leading. I am leading in ways you do not understand—ways you may think are beyond your competence—but you forget that my power is there for you to use and overcome. Overcome the lack of forgiveness. Forgiveness is important to me; this is one key that is needful to bring about your complete victory.*

Father God, as we confess our sins, you delight in forgiving them. Even so, Lord, I'm ashamed of my tortoise-like progress. I've thought I had completely forgiven the one whose actions has caused unquestionable trauma—but obviously by your word, this is not so.

O Lord, wretched me! I pray no unkind thoughts concerning him will enter my mind, and that my heart toward him will soften. This is such a vital thing to conquer. I struggle with forgiveness; this cannot be achieved by my own efforts. The more focused on injuries, the greater the offense is magnified. I request that the Holy Spirit forgive through me. Paul said, "In him we have redemption through his blood, the forgiveness of sins, in accordance with the riches of God's grace that He lavished on us with all wisdom and understanding" (Eph. 1:7–8). It's grace, isn't it, Lord? To grow in grace is to grow like you, Jesus, in countless ways—including forgiveness.

On Christian TV a pastor recounted his vision of heaven and then the fiery furnace of hell. An angel forewarned him, saying, "If you were judged at this moment you would be in this place for all eternity, as you cannot forgive your wife."

Lord, I see in the story of the rich man and Lazarus that the rich man in hell was alert and aware of his surroundings. In hell as in heaven, all the senses are stimulated and the damned remember. It is simple to imagine the anguish of the tormented souls in hell as they recall the chances given them on earth to enter heaven. Instead, they were deaf to the message and turned away to follow the world, ending in the devil's realm. The Bible tells of Adam and Eve, who surrendered to the devil's temptation and lost dominion over the earth to Satan. The devil, the god of this world, deceives and drags into hell all who reject you, Jesus. Once in hell, it's too late to repent or ask forgiveness. It's hard to contemplate the horror of this. Lord Jesus, it perturbs me that manifold folk today are deceived and drawn by Satan's temptations. I pray, Jesus, that countless people will realize and repent before it's too late.

To slay the self within must be the answer, as the dead cannot hurt or be hurt or clamor for their own way. The importance is we must be born again spiritually; you say so in your Word, Jesus. This I perceive, Lord, is the secret: as we die to our self-life, we are able to live our lives in relation to God's commands without our own agenda getting in the way. Again, the Scriptures say: "If we confess our sins, he is faithful and just and will forgive us our sins and purify us from all unrighteousness" (1 John 1:9).

Jesus, there is no problem in forgiving those who we love. With a greater love for mankind in our hearts, it would be much easier to obey your command of love and forgive our enemies as well. I need help, my Lord, to love and pardon the one who has and is causing such heartfelt anguish.

Be kind and compassionate to one another, forgiving each other, just as in Christ God forgave you. (Eph. 4:32)

Do you find it easy to forgive and show empathy for those who mistreat you?

Write your thoughts here.

14

Walking in Love

Be completely humble and gentle; be patient, bearing with one another in love. (Eph. 4:2)

What are ways this love can be shown in your life, so you can bring love into other lives?

This morning, Jesus, I read in Ephesians 5:2 that we are to "live a life of love." My Jesus, it's love; it's all about love. Walking daily in love is a choice to not be immoral, impure, or greedy—rather, to be kind, to think of the other person before self. Jesus, in the daily walk of many citizens throughout the country, I hear coarse joking, idiotic talk, blasphemy, drunkenness, foul language, and debauchery—all that leads to foolishness. Motives matter so deeply; so much depends on our motives. With love in our hearts, it would not be easy to break your holy commandment to love.

Lord, our society today views tolerance as a great virtue, even to the point of becoming tolerant of what you speak against in Scripture. It is important to discern and use wisdom, and to refuse to accept anything and everything dished up in the name of tolerance. Jesus, today people and even some Christians accept that which was frowned upon not too many years earlier. We are labeled bigots and identified as unloving if we speak against what you condemn in your Word. Lord, it is not love when we are pressured to consent to what you speak against, even when they present it in sweet, dignified words. We are to follow your word and use discernment, but most of all to walk in love.

Lord, in my spirit I sense that whatever people say or do to me is unimportant—what is important is that I don't hold hostility toward them in my heart, but turn the other cheek and attempt to love and respect them as your created ones. This is what you taught as you set the example on the cross and said, "Father, forgive them, for they do not know what they are doing" (Luke 23:34). Hurt is real, and often difficult to forgive. But you decreed we are to forgive "not seven times, but seventy-seven times" (Matt. 18:22). This is difficult, Lord—perhaps too difficult! But you, and only you, can give the power, strength, and will to do it. Through the anointing of the Holy Spirit, as we forgive others, you will forgive us. How delightful is that, Lord? Please, Jesus, flood me with love, that I may love those who speak against me.

Speaking of love, Lord, I sorrow when I think of little orphans whom you dearly love. Many fail to receive all the love they deserve. I pray in particular for the millions of orphans whose parents are unable to provide financially for them—and especially, most especially, those little ones who are sold as sex slaves, commodities sold to the highest bidder. O my Lord, what has man become? I pray also for and ask you to protect and bless the courageous people who risk their lives to rescue these dear parentless children from despicable men who use and abuse the innocent, and from those exploiters who greatly enrich themselves through this nefarious trade. Christians need to flood this world with love, so that some may flow over onto these precious little ones.

I pray too for the organizations, the people who care for the rescued orphans. Sadly, there are still too many left to fend for themselves! Dear Jesus, I pray you will inspire numerous Christians around the globe to diligently pray about the reprehensible situations we encounter daily. What a significance impact this would make throughout the world.

Jesus, you have provided sufficient space, food, and natural resources on this planet for all, but human greed and lack of wisdom has caused an imbalance and scarcity, diminishing the quality of life among the poor. This should not be. It's an outcome of this wretched, fallen world. Much love is lacking in the world today. Jesus, it's so important to walk in love.

I weep for the millions upon millions of babes aborted in their mother's womb, these precious ones never given a chance to see daylight. Jesus, I bring the abortionists to you and pray they look to you and comprehend their cruelty. Many in this world acquiesce to the sucking of babes out of their mother's womb limb by limb while their hearts still beat. They can excuse themselves and quiet their conscience that it is legal, but it is not legal in your eyes, Jesus. These little ones you created in your image are so dear to your heart. How it must deeply sadden you, man's inhumanity to man; the cruelty of adults to tiny children tears at my heartstrings.

Child, my heart is torn, too. Do your little bit and leave the rest to me. Spread love abroad; shower it on everyone you encounter. It is love that covers all sin and brings you into a close relationship with me. It is your faith and my power that enables you to do all things through my strength and to overcome the sadness in your heart.

I'm aware I must love my enemy, and the enemies of little babes, but as I have experienced it is not always easy. I believe, Jesus, that love is the fulfilling of the law (Rom. 13:10). As Paul says in Galatians, "Clearly no one is justified before God, by the law, because, "The righteous will live by faith" (Gal. 3:11). And again, Jesus, you said, "The greatest commandant is: 'Love the Lord your God with all your heart and with all your soul and with all your mind.' . . . And the second is like it: 'Love your neighbor as yourself.' All the Law and the Prophets hang on these two commandments" (Matt. 22:37, 39–40). I pray, please fill me with love that I may love my neighbors, whosoever they may be.

I pray that you, being rooted and established in love, may have power, together with all the saints, to grasp how wide and long and high and deep is the love of Christ, and to know this love that surpasses knowledge—that you may be filled to the measure of all the fullness of God. (Eph. 3:17–19)

How wonderful for all saints to grasp this truth. I encourage you to walk in love and note down the significance of this verse to you personally.

Turn the Other Cheek

I tell you, Do not resist an evil person. If someone strikes you on the right cheek, turn to him the other cheek also. (Matt. 5:39)

Weigh up the challenge of this statement.

Thank you, Lord, for endeavoring to teach me to turn the other cheek and forgive. However, Jesus, it seems to me virtually unattainable! Animosity toward the one responsible for our trauma crushes in upon me, particularly when it is ongoing, disturbing my spirit, and rendering me unable to rise above the circumstances. You say, "Love your enemies and pray for those who persecute you" (Matt. 5:44). Lord, I don't feel like loving him, but I do pray for his soul. It's a challenge! I pray I will love him one day with agape love, that pure love that comes from you. If I am honest, Jesus, I have harbored revenge in my heart. Although I have not retaliated, I want him to suffer the consequence of his actions. For this, Jesus, I ask forgiveness. Unconfessed revenge breeds ugly natures within. Pity me, O my God.

Lord Jesus, you are humble, loving, and forgiving. I assume unforgiveness hurts the person exhibiting it more than the person it is directed at. I've heard that revenge is sweet, but I imagine the sweetness would not be long-lasting. If my attitude toward the enemy is one of bitterness and not one of turning the other cheek and forgiveness, then it is I who inflicts suffering upon myself. I must have help not to fall into the devil's trap. I pray the one who has caused such turmoil will be given a revelation of your precious and most powerful love. Love is certainly stronger than evil. It's the soul that is important; revenge could not turn this one to you. Lord, it's vital to obey your Word.

Furthermore, the fact that you teach us to love our enemies is as much for our benefit as for theirs. You use all circumstances to bring forth good, both for the victim and the perpetrator, as you love each equally. You are then able to use us to genuinely witness to our enemy. At the point when he responds and acknowledges you, Lord God, we can both come into the kingdom pure, clean, and rejoicing together. I pray, Lord, that he will be brought to the valley of decision.

With your help I wish to see him differently—not as an enemy but as a miserable and tormented soul, bound and activated by demons, a person in need of compassion and deeply in need of you, Jesus. My forgiveness for him is fragmented. One moment I think I've forgiven him, and the next moment thoughts enter my mind to remind me I haven't! Oh Jesus, I feel mortified. Please help me not to condemn. Instill in me a genuine desire to pray for the salvation of his soul, to turn the other cheek, and to find love for him in my heart. O my Lord, where are you? I feel helpless, even desperate.

My child, I hear you and will do more than you could ever ask. You are in spiritual warfare, so be aware of your enemy and see his hand in your feelings of desperation and in your blindness to my presence, my precious child. Do not sink, but lift your head high and see me, your Lord and friend, beckoning you to leave the world and the concern of what people may say and follow me. It is not difficult, with my help. Simply make up your mind, let go of all, and hand everything over to me. I am in you, and I am greater than the one who is in the world.

You are the Judge, Jesus, and I ask your forgiveness for thoughts of revenge, wishing he get his just deserts, and please help me to turn the other cheek and not live as the world or react as the world but seek the wonders above so as to rise above and beyond all ungodly matters of this planet that disturb my spirit. I thank you and praise you Jesus.

If someone strikes you on the right cheek, turn to him the other also. And if someone wants to sue you and take your tunic, let him have your cloak as well. If someone forces you to go one mile, go with him two miles.
(Matt. 5:39–41)

Reflect on these verses and what they may mean specifically to you.

The Judge

Do not judge, or you too will be judged. For in the same way you judge others, you will be judged, and with the measure you use, it will be measured to you.
(Matt. 7:1–2)

Can you see the benefits of studying this verse and obeying its directive?

Today, Lord, when queried about our situation, I was confronted with a critical and a judgmental attitude. It's a challenge not to let it all out, purely to get it off my chest. Once more, your Word says, "There is only one Lawgiver and Judge. . . . But you—who are you to judge your neighbor?" (James 4:12). Jesus, I realize it is a grave matter to take over your authority, your role.

When I speak against the one who has caused such pain, sadness, and heartache, Lord, I wound you—as you are the universal God whose love is for all people. Any criticism or judgment against one who you created and love is, to you, unkind criticism. You watch and wait for this one to come to you. O Lord, remove the plank from my eye, to see and forgive all. Focus my thoughts upon you, that I may refrain from becoming judgmental.

Lord, many Christians have been judged and deemed unworthy to live by certain nations, and millions have been killed in recent years. We hear little of this in the mainstream media. Lord, are Christians expendable in their eyes? I discern the time is coming when many of those who love you in western countries may be persecuted, misunderstood, judged, mocked, beaten, and discriminated against. Even some Christians will stand by in silence, as happened during the Holocaust. We should when necessary, Jesus, speak out against injustice as we see it. But to please you, we must not avenge ourselves or stand in judgment of others. You have told us to turn the other cheek (Matt. 5:39). You, precious Jesus, are our avenger and judge. Indeed, we must forgive and forget, but sometimes, Lord, this is exceedingly challenging, particularly when the situation is ongoing.

Lord, the news is distressing, such horrors worldwide; I pray I won't miss the trumpet call. My view is that we are leading up to the great tribulation; much is being readied for the entrance and welcome of the Antichrist. I'm sure many in this world will welcome him with open arms and with joy and even worship him as God. What a terrifying shock to these poor deceived deluded people at the day of judgment when you, Jesus, sit on your throne to judge all. I pray not to fall into the devil's trap but to obey your instructions. You say in your Word, "Be perfect, therefore, as your heavenly Father is perfect" (Matt. 5:48). Why did you put that in the Scriptures? For me, Jesus, it's too hard! It's not always trouble-free being a Christian.

Lord, before I became a Christian, I judged that I was righteous. Even long afterward, it was easy for me to find excuses and rationalize my misdemeanors, or even be blind to them and thus refrain from honestly judging myself. But the closer I grow to you, the more the imperfections within reveal themselves, and this bothers me. I ask forgiveness, Father, in Jesus' name.

We all must judge ourselves with sincerity and frankness. I pray, Lord, that when we are misjudged, we will not be moved nor harden our hearts against those who judge us but be forgiving and gracious. Heaven forbid that we should judge them; please save us from that, dear Jesus. I sense too, Lord, that it's more challenging for people who see ourselves as righteous to humble ourselves and commit our lives under your control. We all are in need of help, Jesus! I find it's not easy to live up to your lofty rules. I sense my lapses, and particularly my sin of criticism and my judgmental attitude, create a distance between us.

> *My child, there is no distance between us, as I've told you many times. Remember that I am still within you, to guide you and protect you and lead you along the path.*

I thank you that you chose not to remember for all eternity the sins that have been confessed and forgiven. It's not you, Lord Jesus, it's me. It's me who finds it difficult to forgive myself. I fall into the evil one's trap. I have to be careful that I don't lessen the impact of your sacrifice or take away from it; you died for the sins of all people. All we need to do is to accept it and realize that sins forgiven will not be judged; instead, Christians will be judged for rewards. Is that correct, Lord?

Lord Jesus, I'm grateful that I need not fear your judgment. You are our ultimate judge, and will judge with justice and integrity. Jesus, you're so good! You see the best in everyone, and you don't judge during this age of grace. You simply love. Judgment will come about at the end of the age—but even then, it will be fair, as you can judge no other way. Lord, how great you are!

But I tell you that men will have to give an account on the day of judgment for every careless word they have spoken. (Matt. 12:36)

This should cause shame about the careless words we speak.

Write down your personal thoughts on hurtful words you have spoken, and seek forgiveness from or forgive others who have spoken hurtful words to you.

Praise Jesus, who died for the sins committed through those words.

_____
_____
_____
_____
_____
_____
_____
_____
_____
_____
_____
_____
_____
_____

Eternity

Whoever believes in the Son has eternal life, but whoever rejects the Son will not see life, for God's wrath remains on him. (John 3:36)

What picture comes to your mind as you read this verse?

Lord, when I ponder eternity, what is persecution, anguish, or wounds if our tormentor can escape hellfire and be safe in your kingdom? That would be of all importance, would it not? I can look back on the offenses throughout eternity—if one does look back—and think, "How trivial." You love our tormentor. You wait for him to look up, see you in all your majesty as King, and claim you as his Redeemer, rather than be incarcerated in the pit forever. Such a terrifying place! I do not want him there.

Jesus, the health-and-wealth gospel today is not necessarily protection from adverse circumstances, is it? But this gospel would attract him, as his god is money. I pray when and if he does search for you, Jesus, he will search more in the spiritual realm than the physical. People like him, Lord, who don't heed your Word, end up in the fiery pit of hell and spend forever in this horrendous place, the lake of fire, for all eternity.

Your Word says, "Satan himself masquerades as an angel of light" (2 Cor. 11:14). That is pretence; instead of spreading light, he spreads darkness and deception. He deceives the world; he came to kill, steal, and destroy. You, Lord, gave all a free will; we all choose where we spend eternity. We have only two choices: Jesus or Satan, heaven or hell!

Satan steals our paradise if he beckons us into hell with momentary wealth and temptations of all that glitter in this world. Sadly, those who are lured and dazzled by this transitory illusion will be judged by the Judge. I ask again for your grace to fill me with compassion and forgiveness, even for the tormentor. I pray he will be delivered from insecurities, fears, and hatred—all of which motivate him to hold power and control over others. When he comes to you, Lord, I have confidence he will be a mighty man of valor. What a miracle when his wealth, energy, brainpower, and determination is all directed toward the work of your kingdom! Lord, I do not wish to fall into the trap of retaliation. Please help me and keep me from this, and forgive me. The importance is to pray with the expectation of seeing him eternally in heaven—that Almighty God should be a feeling of great pleasure.

Lord, this morning as I continued to pray for this one who has caused such grief, I saw a vision: A deep dark hole, and a gigantic black spider being drawn into it. As I looked up, I saw a mountain, and atop this mountain within sight was a bright shining castle with its flag flying in the breeze. I knew that the spider represented our tormentor, being dragged down into the abyss by the evil one. I needed to pray earnestly for him to gaze up and see the castle where your flag flies high, and to choose between the dominion of darkness and the pristine light of your kingdom—the kingdom that shines with the glory of God with a brilliance unknown on earth. Much within is pure gold as pure as crystal; the hearts that dwell there are purified by the Holy Spirit. Holy Jesus, I thank you for that vision how wonderful and glorious! I ask that you bless the tormentor abundantly. Please, Holy Spirit, draw him to yourself, where he can find forgiveness and be forever in paradise. I pray he will not go into the fiery pit of hell, a place of eternal torment. My prayer is he may demonstrate real penitence and be purified and forgiven before judgment. Lord Jesus, I have many in my family who do not believe in an afterlife nor have a belief in you; I pray the same for them. I fear they have no comprehension of the soul. I pray they will realize the body is not really them; it is physical. It comes from dust and will return to dust. The soul is spiritual and comes from above and is eternal. I pray they will come to the realization that there is more to this life than the physical, that the body is the house we live in during our earthly walk; it enables us to connect to the physical world. The soul is who we are. I pray their eyes will be opened, and that they will repent and ask forgiveness, then come into your kingdom and spend eternity in that beautiful place of radiance and splendor, heaven. Hell is too horrendous to consider. But if they do not choose you, Lord, then their choice is hell, and they will hear these terrible words:

Depart from me, you who are cursed, into the eternal fire prepared for the devil and his angels. (Matt. 25:41)

What startling challenge do you see in these final words?

Purify My Heart

Create in me a pure heart, O God, and renew a steadfast spirit within me. (Ps. 51:10)

Is your aim transformation? Have you considered purification, or counted the cost?

This verse above, Jesus, is likewise my request. But it is difficult to believe the time it has taken to forgive the one who has wreaked such havoc. I need my heart purified. I struggle to refrain from wanting him to pay the penalty. Lord, it hasn't been just to endure it all these years. But when I reflect upon the brutal suffering you endured on the cross for the whole world, my situation looks insignificant. I'm deeply in need of your pardon, Lord.

Yes, my child, that person has said and done hurtful things; but what is that to you? You wound me when you criticize one whom I love dearly.

In your kindness, Lord, you endeavor to make me see the truth in your Word, "For our struggle is not against flesh and blood, but against the rulers, against the authorities, against the powers of this dark world and against the spiritual forces of evil in the heavenly realms" (Eph. 6:12). Jesus, it is forever between me and evil. Help me, Lord, to be conscious of this verse at all times, so as not have adverse feelings against the human who Satan works through.

As for me, Lord—purify my heart. May your pure love flow through me, then overflow toward that person who has caused such devastation. I wanted purification without the pain. In my own frail heart, I have wished for a comfortable life, a respite from life's sufferings, the tyranny, and the harsh testing. But my way is not your way. Your aim is to bring holiness into our lives so as to become pure in heart. Please, I pray, sanctify all who read this and deliver them from the evil one and assist them to obey your statutes. I pray too, Lord, that I become merciful, compassionate, and unselfish toward others and kept from worldliness. Jesus, your patience with me is beyond comprehension.

I read in *As a Man Thinketh*: "The sole and supreme use of suffering is to purify, to burn out all that is useless and impure. Suffering ceases for him who is pure. There could be no object in burning gold after the dross had been removed."[3] That's it, isn't it, Lord? You watch to see your children's hearts purified. This fleeting life and strife we are now living is preparation for eternal life in heaven. I pray for purification. I believe it is suffering that purifies.

Lord Jesus, I give you my heart. I take comfort in your Word. I give thanks to you for the miracles. I trust there is a marvelous purpose for everything you allow to touch us, no matter how difficult. Our task is to love and pardon those whose grievous attempts are to wound. Help us, Lord, to comply with your wishes and to endeavor to keep our hearts pure, as you are pure, so that we may set an example in ministry that creates everlasting eternal influences.

Don't let anyone look down on you because you are young, but set an example for the believers in speech, in life, in love, in faith and in purity. (1 Tim. 4:12)

This advice applies to all ages. What steps could you take to live up to the advice Paul gave Timothy?

Ministry

But you, keep your head in all situations, endure hardship, do the work of an evangelist, discharge all the duties of your ministry. (2 Tim. 4:5)

All this is from God, who reconciled us to himself through Christ and gave us the ministry of reconciliation. (2 Cor. 5:18)

Can you visualize what your ministry will be like in five years?

Father God, I pray in the name of Jesus that our ministries and witness will reconcile countless folk to you. However, Lord God, I fear no ministry can be truly powerful without abiding prayer. Nor can it be spiritual if we are not guided daily by the Holy

Spirit. I give you thanks, Jesus, for the special talents and gifts given to enable each to perform the ministry you have designed exclusively for us—that you said no other individual would be as adequate to achieve. Lord, I envisage it is surely beneficial also to appraise our prayer life periodically.

> *Child, go forth walking in the light, your hand in mine, going not before me and not behind me, but with me all the way. I go hand in hand with you, and yet as you exercise your calling and ministry, I also go before you and prepare hearts. As well, I stay behind you, completing the work that you began.*

You, Jesus, are not limited by time and space. Sometimes I hear people say that God doesn't work that way or this way. You may not work that way with them, but this does not limit you from working any way you please with others. Each ministry is unique. Lord Jesus, please assist me to follow your guidance at all times, as I wish not to dishonor your name. Thus, Lord, I aspire to set my affections on things above, not on the things of this earth. Today I pray, Jesus, please sustain me so I may overcome my weariness.

> *My child, keep praising and worshiping me. This is the only way your ministry will be fruitful, by looking to me and keeping close to me. You are blessed indeed to know you are in this very position, although you may*

feel drained and exhausted at times; remember, that is how I felt in the garden of Gethsemane. You are exceedingly precious to me. I love you and notwithstanding feeling low as you did today, you achieved a great work for me. This can only be done for those who I bring across your path. Never go out looking for who to speak to. You know how words flow when you are led completely by the Spirit. Some I give the gift of speaking in public, others witness here and there whenever they consider someone needs to be spoken to. My dear one, keep on as you are going and many will be blessed.

You said, Jesus, "The harvest is plentiful, but the workers are few. Ask the Lord of the harvest, therefore, to send out workers into his harvest field" (Luke 10:2). I pray that we will all be awakened to the harvest that is ready to be brought in; there is a great need for us to be ready for this work. I'm grateful that your design for this world included plans specially tailored to suit each individual. This life is all about you, Jesus. Our highest blessing is to know you, my Lord, and to minister unto others as you direct.

People need to be prepared, to be spiritually ready for the harvest. Your ministry is to bring it in. Please don't rush ahead of me!

Yes Lord, I wish to keep in step with you and not wander from the blueprint, your roadmap. Jesus, it's sad some pastors are not pleasing you. They are not always walking the path their ministry dictates. They fail to speak out against corruption or make leaders in high places accountable for their actions. Church leaders have a responsibility to speak out against what you, God, speak out against in the Bible. Had all believers been faithful in doing so, many anti-Christian policies today would have failed to become law, I believe we have all failed to a degree in this endeavor. Some church leaders water down the Word, which dilutes the power of the gospel. They fear to upset their parishioners, so they speak out nice-sounding words with no Holy Spirit authority behind them. They tickle their listeners' itching ears, which give a nice warm fuzzy feeling but no gospel power (2 Tim. 4:3). The result is that prayer is lacking, zeal is deficient, and the gospel weakened. Dear Jesus, this does not create purified hearts. Prayer is such an important aspect of our ministry. We should value it above all other activities.

The real sermon is made in the closet. The man—God's man—is made in the closet. . . . Every preacher who does not make prayer a mighty factor in his own life and ministry is weak as a factor in God's work and is powerless to advance God's cause in this world.[4]

Do you pray for the ministry of another? Does a prayer intercessor pray for your ministry? Who could you add to your prayer list for this undertaking, and what specifically would require prayer?

Security

"Take a guard," Pilate answered. "Go, make the tomb as secure as you know how." (Matt. 27:65)

No man can secure what Jesus does not want secured. We see this when Peter was rescued from prison by the angel (Acts 12:6-17). Deliberate upon this and think about where your security lies.

Lord, I've continuously wished to live in security, but I sense you desire to take me out into utter insecurity so as to completely rely on you. After all, that's what I'm beginning to believe genuine security really is—total reliance on you.

Father, may your Holy Spirit enable me to live according to your commands. Your commands do not bind but as we follow them we enjoy liberty, and in your liberty is security. Jesus, as I walk in the Spirit of love—to love you, my friends, and even as you command, my enemy—may you open up the opportunity to share your precious Word with others, so you may be to them a protective and secure haven. I pray they will be inspired to give you the love and worship which is so pleasing to you.

My child, I want you to open up to me. Open your eyes to see the light, your ears to hear my voice, and your heart to accept my love and release your tongue to speak my words. You are so dear to me, my precious child.

Jesus, my expectation is to do as you ask. As I awake and prepare for the day, I rejoice in you. There are manifold matters demanding my attention, including a garden party—but we all need to keep our eyes on you, and our hearts and ears attuned to you for guidance in the midst of the most crowded day, to see opportunities to serve you in every interruption.

Your ministry can be diverse, so as you say, my child, be prepared in the midst of your crowded day.

It is you who inspires our work, so help us, Lord, to let go and let God. Security is found only in you. By our faith and your power, miracles occur. I pray to be safe and secure in your arms and my witness fully directed by your Holy Spirit.

Jesus, I do at times fail in the midst of the complexities set before me.

> *My child, you must not look at yourself. You fail when you take your eyes off me. Remember, I forgave your failings; they have been nailed to the cross. Do not be too introspective, but look out toward your fellow man and see how you can help.*

Jesus, I am reminded of Peter when he walked on the water. He was safe and secure, but once his eyes came off you and became conscious of the waves, he began to sink. Help me, Lord, to keep my eyes on you, as that is my only sanctuary. Some people today look to money for security, but real security is found only within the refuge you so generously provide.

Because God wanted to make the unchanging nature of his purpose very clear to the heirs of what was promised, he confirmed it with an oath. God did this so that, by two unchangeable things in which it is impossible for God to lie, we who have fled to take hold of the hope offered to us may be greatly encouraged. We have this hope as an anchor for the soul, firm and secure.
(Heb. 6:17–19)

This gives confidence in the security of Jesus' promise and engenders absolute trust in him. How can you obtain comfort from this verse?

21

Money

The love of money is a root of all kinds of evil.
(1 Tim. 6:10)

If you were in a position of authority, how would you overcome this issue of money in the world? Evaluate this problem.

Lord, with love taken out of the equation, money is useful for daily living and multiple needs in the world. Yet the love of money has been the cause of horrendous tragedies. How I need your wisdom in learning how to manage it in ways that please you! I previously focused on being a good steward, but hesitated to spend and became instead a hoarder. Ill-advised, I've twice lost abundant sums through erroneous investments.

> *My child, your focus was more on your finances than on me. With the loss of your money, you turned back to me.*

I pray my time and my resources, little as they are, will be at your disposal in the future for those in need. Lord, you are the Great Giver. Please forgive me for my stinginess; I'm mindful that ungenerous giving dwarfs the soul. My lack of funds at times troubles me, but I pray to become more generous with my finances in the future. I tithe and give offerings, but not as cheerfully as you direct—"God loves a cheerful giver" (2 Cor. 9:7). I genuinely pray, Jesus, that I will not be enslaved to money nor obsessed with possessions.

> *My child, I see there is not much money pouring into your life. It may seem to you a little frugal, but in that is the greatest treasure you could find, because you know how to call on me, your Father, to be your provider.*

Thank you, Jehovah Jiveh, I see that having money is unimportant. Money doesn't satisfy; the more one has, the more one wants. If my needs are met, Lord, then money is inconsequential. I would rather have the greatest treasure.

> *As you are aware, my child, when you are holding on to something I need you to relinquish, you have no hands to hold that which I wish to shower down upon you. Release all*

to me, and you will be filled. Do not worry about your finances; hand all over to me, and all will be well.

Lord, speaking lately to you about my resources, I remarked, "little as they are. A quote from *I Heard Heaven Proclaim* says that negative comments bring about the spirit of poverty upon finances, for example, "We don't have enough money for this or that" or "We can't afford to pay him that much!"[5] In turn, the spirit of poverty I believe means we have less to give. Jesus, we need to watch the words we speak forth. I pray that the pleasure of giving for your purposes will become a living reality within me. You said, "It is more blessed to give than to receive" (Acts 20:35). These are wise words.

Child, I love you dearly and I want you to give money to my work here. You are so precious to me. I have great plans for you, plans you know not of at this stage. You should always gain much from me in these quiet times alone and go forth empowered and blessed by me to bless others. Your work is only starting; there is much for you to do. Keep yourself free to do this and do not become overburdened with things of this world. This is not for you; you have a greater purpose in this life than gaining worldly possessions. Know I am able to do all things beyond what you can ever imagine.

Jesus, I need to surrender my money. Aid me to give and enjoy giving for the sake of the kingdom. You say, "No one can serve two masters. Either he will hate the one and love the other . . . You cannot serve both God and Money" (Matt. 6:24). So I shall serve you, Lord. I wish to serve you as Peter and John did at the beautiful gate, when the crippled man begged for money. Peter said, "Silver or gold I do not have, but what I have I give you. In the name of Jesus Christ of Nazareth, walk" (Acts 3:6). In this situation, Lord, I see the man's need was not for continual charity, but for strong legs which would enable him to earn his living for the entirety of his life.

Last week, Lord, you spoke of my little mite, mentioning how mighty it is in your kingdom. I'm reminded of the loaves and fish, and I thank you for multiplying my gift.

I thank you, Jesus, that whatever your requirement of me is, there's always ample money to accomplish it. In fact, I can live without asking whether I can afford this or that. As I pray and intercede for finances, you enable me not to feel impoverished but to realize I'm abundantly enriched. Lord Jesus, I appreciate your gifts, both material and spiritual.

Whoever loves money never has money enough; whoever loves wealth is never satisfied with his income. (Eccl. 5:10)

Honestly speaking, what is the most important thing in your life? If you could choose one thing, what would it be?

Intercession

Prayer! What exactly is it? Basically, prayer is the simplest act a creature of God can perform. It is divine communion with our heavenly father.[6]

Consistency in prayer is the evidence of true commitment.[7]

Can you honestly say that this is your commitment?

Prayer, in my case, is just chatting to you, Lord Jesus. Prayer can be our deepest expression to you; but it needs to be sincere and honest, as you know all our thoughts and each and every motive. We cannot deceive you.

This morning I'm reminded of what you said to me recently: "Your work is that of an intercessor." Heavenly Father, this is a great privilege! I ask for the zeal needed to carry out this ministry. Prayer is serious work; it can determine the path we take, likewise that of our families and leaders of countries when prayed according to your will. Please, Lord, help me; to be lax in prayer is to fail in these endeavors.

Dear Jesus, first of all I wish to intercede for my family. I'm reminded that it is you who works mightily in their lives. I ask that you lead godly, Spirit-filled Christians to witness to those who do not know you and to strengthen those who do. Within your Word, Father, you have given each of these beautiful people keys to open the doors into the kingdom. The first key is choice. I pray they will choose Jesus instead of Satan, heaven instead of hell, life instead of death, light instead of darkness, glory instead of dishonor, joy instead of sorrow, and victory instead of defeat. This life is a parenthesis; the best is still to come, is it not so?

> *Yes, my child, the best is yet to come! This world as it is will not last. Hold onto what is eternal. Your children will be touched by me again; I keep building upon these times when they are touched. I promise you again, my child: they will come to me. How blessed are those who have praying parents! Hold up all your loved ones together to me. When prayer is needed for them separately, I will inform you.*

Jesus, I ask the Holy Spirit to speak into the hearts of all on my prayer list who do not know you. My aspiration is that they not only know *about you* but know you personally. I pray they will seek that all-embracing love that radiates from you. My request is that you reveal yourself to them and open their eyes to see your love, your kingdom, and eternal purposes. Please, Holy Spirit, encourage them to seek forgiveness, repent, and completely surrender control of their lives into your hands, so that they may be saved from the blazing pit of hell.

Lord, I need your help again. I still seem to fail in my witness. Please help me.

My child, you were perfectly in my will. The words that you spoke today will come back to this person. I will bring them back to her mind. You were persecuted for my sake, my child. I love you; you are incredibly precious to me. Keep trusting me and resting in me. I have a powerful work for you to do in the future. My child, I love hearing you discuss my Word; it is precious to me. I am building you up in the Spirit, which is soon to be released.

Lord, you have instilled within me a great yearning for all my friends as I intercede for them to come into a deep-seated relationship with you. I wish to save them the years it has taken me to grow to a measure of spiritual maturity. I appreciate you as you work in the hearts of people who have not completely come out of the world. May they all accept the precious gift of salvation you so freely give.

Be a light shining on the mountaintops, showing the way to me, and I will set them free.

How magnificent, Lord. Freedom is peace, that peace that passes all understanding. At times, Jesus, we come to you as little children—I want, I want, give me, give me! You wish us all to come to you as little children, not in that sense but in the sense of the pure faith of a child. It is so precious to quietly sit alone with you, Jesus, not asking anything of you but simply enjoying your presence. I intercede again for family and relatives those who don't know you. I pray merely for what will benefit their spiritual development. I ask that they realize and experience your great love and mighty power and look up and see you in all your glory.

> *Daughter, when you pray for others, pray in the name of Jehovah El-Elohe Israel. Personalize the person's name in place of "Israel," because I am your personal God.*

I pray for all my friends to become friends of God. It's amazing and so joyful to spend time in prayer and meditate upon you. The closer we come to you, the greater the joy we find in you. How impressive is that? Jesus, you spent much time in prayer while on earth. I pray we will heed your example.

Jesus went out to a mountainside to pray, and spent the night praying to God. (Luke 6:12)

Think about ways your prayer life can be improved and zeal increased.

Eyes on You

The eyes of the Lord are on the righteous and his ears are attentive to their prayer, but the face of the Lord is against those who do evil. (1 Pet. 3:12)

As you consciously strive to keep your eyes upon Jesus, can you contemplate in your mind's eye the shekinah glory of God?

I glorify you Jesus, our Great High Priest, the light of the world who intercedes for us! I come to you in prayer this morning; I thank you for your gift of joy. I honor you as I enjoy your presence. Lord, as I keep my eyes upon you, I am so abundantly blessed.

I am blessed by your presence too, my child.

Jesus, it is a mystery to me how I can bless you! However, I will trust your Word. Each time I come into your presence for prayer or merely sit in silence with you, we are both blessed. Jesus, in prayer I'm discovering that listening is an important aspect of it; in particular, it helps me to keep my eyes totally focused on you. Humans are not apt at listening, as often we're anxious to get a word in and express our own opinions. I'm shockingly bad at this. On the other hand, prayer takes our attention off self, provided we listen attentively to the voice of the Holy Spirit and keep our eyes on you, just as your eyes are constantly focused upon us.

Some Christians mentioned the difficulties they have in hearing the inner voice of the Holy Spirit. I read an answer you gave Marie Shropshire in her book *In Touch with God*, which speaks clearer than I could:

> Your first step was taken in the direction of understanding how to enter my silence when you *desired* stillness. Many so-called desires are passing whims. When the desire of the heart is in harmony with the language of the mouth, the desire is sincere. The sincere desire is rewarded because it diligently seeks its object. You are seeking you shall find. . . . Sense my presence; be conscious of the love flowing from me to you. Pure, unconditional love emanates from my being. Drink in that love. Remain in that state of quietness as long as possible, Silence any wandering thoughts. After several days of practicing such periods of uninterrupted quietude, you will begin to hear my voice rather than your own.[8]

"My sheep listen to my voice" (John 10:27).

Seek always to be in the habit of prayer. Always have your eyes and your mind focused on me, and then you cannot walk contrary to my will.

Lord, please forgive me. My attempts to stay my mind on you and my eyes upon you and my ears open to hear are often ineffective. I have difficulty praying unceasingly; at the same time, when alone, this problem still often persists.

My child, when you have your eyes and mind thoroughly focused on the task before you, my Spirit prays within you. Notice how it is that as you finish an assignment you are fully absorbed in; your mind instantly returns to me. I am aware that you are not only a spiritual person but contained within a fleshly body. Keep persevering as you have been doing, my beloved.

Please intercede for me, Lord Jesus, so I may acquire success in stilling my thoughts, focus totally on you, and become victorious in our quiet times alone.

Only rest in me. My Spirit is at work within you to do what you are unable to do.

Dear Jesus, in our prayer times together, you teach about letting go and point out why I pray about different points. You have pointed out hints of selfishness in requests and the wrong motives behind them. You have reminded me that the fear of the Lord is the beginning of wisdom. I pray, Lord, that fear will drive me to keep my eyes upon you and my ears attentive to your still, small voice—that it will give me the wisdom to walk in your ways as King David did, who said, "My eyes are ever on the LORD" (Ps. 25:15).

Jesus, I pray that as the glory of God is revealed, my worldly mind transformed, and turbulent emotions repaired and made whole, you will enhance my capacity to intercede for the needs of those you show me. Lord, it is good to keep our eyes on you and hold tightly to you and not let go. You always had your eyes on the Father, and at the same time were aware of your disciples' earthly needs.

Do you have eyes but fail to see, and ears but fail to hear?
And don't you remember?
When I broke the five loaves for the five thousand. . . .
Do you still not understand?
(Mark 8:18–19, 21)

Reflect on ways you can keep your eyes upon Jesus at all times so you may see and understand. Thank him in writing that he, too, has his eyes upon you.

Wider Intercession

*Intercession is much more than merely praying for others.
Intereeding is engaging in actual battle.⁹*

Appraise your prayer life and consider
this law.

Intercessory prayer is a blessed favor conferred on us by you, Lord. I'm unsure if we all appreciate this. Our laziness must, to a certain degree, cause slackness in our prayer life. Yet we are involved in spiritual warfare. Many times, we must wrestle with Satan and his entities that come against us; their sole aim is to prevent humans from coming to you, Jesus. If he fails in this purpose, he ventures to hinder the Christian's prayer life with attempts to make us ineffective in prayer and in ministry. I pray he will not succeed!

Father God, I pray for and bring to you in Jesus' name the dedicated pastors who faithfully preach your Word. I ask that you anoint them abundantly. I pray for the missionaries, those who give so generously and selflessly of their time to bring others into your kingdom. Please bless these precious people as they work tirelessly to see suffering alleviated and souls saved.

Jesus, I intercede for the residents of the aged homes. Many in their twilight years are unconcerned about their future destination, and this grieves my soul. I again pray in your precious name, Jesus, for those who do not pray for themselves. I ask as I speak to these dear people of your wonderful love, provision, and care that their eyes will open; I long for them to see you in a different light, as the light of the world.

My child, you are a joy to my heart. You have no idea how beautiful it is for me to hear you speaking of me and my love for mankind. Precious daughter, you are resting in me. If all my children would enjoy an intimate relationship with me, I would bless all abundantly through your word and through your witness.

The power of prayer is so powerful and miraculous, Lord Jesus; how brilliant it is to receive a real anointing and fervent spirit for prayer and to see others become prayer intercessors. I ask you to instill courage in us who desire to stand against worldly ways and ideas and not be intimidated, but to speak your words in confidence and witness when directed. I pray we will not be silenced by fear of opposition or fear of what others may think.

My beloved daughter, I want you to take seriously what you have been discussing today. My child, there is a great work ahead of you. Your real work is only beginning. You feel you had a dry time, but this has been an important time when you learned discipline. My hand is heavily upon you; you will have many loving friends in your church. Learn to trust me, always be obedient, and "let go and let God." Always in all things, relax and stop striving!

Lord, it is true. Forgive me, and assist me to "let go and let God." I wish to intercede for Christians who are struggling, and for those who are crying out for help but know not where to go—as well to intercede for those who are comfortable in their wealth, certain ones who are indifferent to the gospel and feel in need of nothing. I pray, Lord, that you would open the eyes of these people to look up and see you—then to see the atrocities throughout the world. Open their hearts and use their wealth and time to alleviate, to best of their ability, some of the incalculable miseries and contribute to making this world a kinder and gentler place. Dear Jesus, I believe the church could play a more powerful role if prayer were its primary goal; what a significant change would be made.

E. M. Bounds wrote, "What the church needs today is not more machinery or better, not new organizations or more and novel methods, but men whom the Holy Spirit can use—men of prayer, men mighty in prayer. The Holy Spirit does not flow through methods but through men."[10] Lord Jesus, you gave me visions of people I knew; now you show me people I do not know. Are they real?

> Yes, my child. Pray for whoever I show you. You may not know their need, but my Heavenly Father knows.

In a vision, I saw the face of a mentally disabled child. Lord, I pray and intercede for the intellectually challenged. I ask on their behalf in your name, Jesus, that you will open the eyes of Christian people near these treasured ones to see that although they may not always understand mentally, spiritually they can. Everyone can look to you, Jesus. That is all it takes—one look with a fervent desire to find you, and they will find you. Thank you, Lord, for showing me they must not be put aside but prayed for and witnessed to and taught so they may be brought into your kingdom renewed and made whole. I intercede once more for the physically challenged, these people beyond doubt are genuinely an inspiration; the herculean feats that many accomplish are astounding. I ask you, precious Jesus, to abundantly bless them, and I pray that many may be drawn into your kingdom and become your friends—the most astounding accomplishment of all. I pray, with this significant change, that miracles will occur.

When I kneel in prayer and with thee, Oh, God, I commune as friend with friend.[11]

Countless souls are seeking a deep and meaningful life. Does your prayer list comprise people such as this? Jot down a short prayer for them.

Significance

To generate a significant difference in the world, the call to Christians in these last days is to gain a greater burden to become intercessors.

Consider the significance of becoming a prayer warrior.

Lord, I understand more and more how powerful prayer is. When praying according to your will, one person in prayer can move leaders and alter situations in faraway nations. At one time, I had an impulse to donate to a worldwide charity. Sadly, I knew my little mite would do naught to alleviate the needs I saw, and I prayed that someone would add to it. Then a vision appeared of an office in a foreign country; I observed a person writing a check for a significance amount to this same mission. Lord, I sincerely thank you for answering that prayer and adding to my mite.

I look ahead to your rule and yearn for the paradise you first created. I'm sure this is what you are working toward—your final plan for mankind. Jesus, I pray for those who are so taken up with the affairs of this world, those who have little time to contemplate the real issues of life and lack the desire to seek you and be ready for your return. My heart yearns for these people, and I say to them, please wake up! My prayer is that your Holy Spirit continues to strive within their hearts. Almighty God, what a huge significance we could together achieve as we all call upon your power in prayer. As your Word says, "Now to him who is able to do immeasurably more than all we ask or imagine, according to his power that is at work within us" (Eph. 3:20).

Jesus, I see prayer is actually a significant weapon gifted to us. As you are well aware, Lord, I undervalued prayer in the early days. As it is purely performed in private, intercession brings no acclamation or credit. Healings or miracles are more spectacular and exciting—but Lord, is this not just pride? It's foolishness to look to the world for recognition or praise; but to look to you in prayer brings greater wisdom and greater impact.

Sometimes I am at a loss, Lord, to know how to pray. On occasion I'm requested to pray for what I see as contrary to your will or selfish insignificant desires, but as I pray in the Spirit, I believe the Spirit intercedes for us with groans that words cannot express. Jesus, I failed to understand the purpose of speaking in the heavenly prayer language, but now realize it's more than the edification of ourselves. As stated in 1 Corinthians 14:4, "He who speaks in a tongue edifies himself." As your Spirit prays within me, I am assured that I am praying according to your will!

Jesus, I discovered multitudes of benefits I had been blind to. As the Holy Spirit speaks directly to our spirits, we are personally edified, but we also gain more insight to more meaningfully help those you bring across our path. This impacts them and makes a significant difference in their lives. Paul spoke to the brothers in Colossae and affirmed his estimation of Epaphras: "Epaphras, who is one of you and a servant of Jesus Christ, sends greetings. He is always wrestling in prayer for you, that you may stand firm in all the will of God, mature and fully assured. I vouch for him that he is working hard for you and those at Laodicea" (Col. 4:12–13). Lord, if there were more people like Epaphras in our world today, what a great increase would be made for the kingdom of God!

Apart from group prayer meetings, the prayer ministry is a solitary path. Jesus, without you, it would be a lonely one. The most inspirational prayer is in the secret place with you—not only in supplication, but simply resting in you.

The greatest significance is found in solitude with Jesus. Do you find solitude pleasant or unpleasant? Do you wrestle in prayer for your loved ones?

Busyness

Getting to know Jesus is to sit in his presence, to talk to him and learn from him. Nevertheless, busyness steals the most precious part of our day. Do you find busyness to be a problem in your prayer life?

Lord, I've been so busy being a people-pleaser. My need is to put up boundaries, discipline myself, and declare: No! Jesus, you divinely planned my journey; it constantly delights me that you continue to walk by my side. With you, I will not falter but will keep on, not considering the path but simply trusting that you know the way, planned from the beginning of time.

Lord, I should not be diligently chasing money. I sometimes become so busy that I rob myself of the time needed to sit quietly with you, and sadly miss out on the precious joy of communion. As I take time off, I dwell upon you and envisage your humility. You came of your own free will; you walked along the path of obedience to death on the cross. You defeated mankind's greatest enemy, Satan. You conquered death and won the victory. You took our punishment upon yourself and opened up the way for us. I am eternally grateful and discern that without you we would all be eternally lost in sin.

It's busyness that cheats us of time with you, Jesus. I thank you for the redemption you earned for mankind. You could have called a legion of angels to come to your rescue, or you could have simply stepped off the cross yourself—nothing is beyond your reach. Nothing or no one has the ability to defeat you. You are undefeatable. There is nothing you cannot do. Actually, in saying that, there *is* something you cannot do—and that is, fail. You forfeited everything for us. I wonder what areas of our lives we would be prepared to give up for you?

Jesus, a vision appeared to me last night in which you revealed a river flowing beside my bedside. As I looked over the edge, a beaver thrust his head up out of the water. I instantly knew the message you desired to convey: "As busy as a beaver." I was *too* busy. The vision clearly communicated a need to delete some programs and tasks from my schedule, to erect boundaries, and to seek you first, before agreeing to further demands. Consequently, I call upon you to give me discernment in my choices. I pray to avoid the insignificant and superficial and choose that which is noteworthy. But you, Lord, are able to bend time and arrange events to suit our timetables when you perceive it necessary. You did this for Joshua—although I am not asking you to make the sun stand still!

Dear Jesus, the frenzy of this world sometimes leaves me reeling. Time in this hectic world is valuable; I comprehend that I need to make a sacrifice of my moments. Yesterday I woke late and rushed through the morning's readings. I promised myself I would meet with you later in the day for what I call my "formal time," but this did not happen. Had I not been in such haste, more would have been accomplished. You were correct when you spoke of resting in you, as this is a time of healing and restoration. Haste cannot bring about renewal.

My child, haste cannot achieve anything. If only you had waited. I waited for you.

I'm so sorry, Jesus; please forgive me. We need to put aside our busyness, especially our preoccupations with novel ideas, and sit and commune awhile in prevailing prayer with you, seeking your guidance in overcoming obsession with things that steal our time.

Busyness is a barrier to prayer. With eyes on the journey with God, the busyness and anxiousness disperse and other responsibilities fade in importance.

What are your thoughts on busyness? Is there a deficiency in your prayer life because of this problem?

Healing

A cheerful heart is good medicine. (Prov. 17:22)

In relation to pain, how does this sentence challenge you?

Jesus, I pray and intercede for those who are desperately in need of healing—physically, mentally, and emotionally. My prayer, Lord, is that the Holy Spirit will intercede to produce great and miraculous healings. I too require healing, Lord. I give my pain over to you, as I know that sickness and pain are not your will. They are not from you, Jesus, but largely from sin or Satan. I confess any unconfessed sin in my life and ask for your forgiveness. May I cast upon you every handicap, every infirmity, for healing. You are my Father God—Jehovah Rophe—the great physician.

Jesus, at church I received healing for Crohn's disease, but very much later it shocked me to feel the same symptoms return. Satan can bring these symptoms back. I am sorry that I believed the lie that I wasn't actually healed. I recognize now that once the lie is believed and accepted, the disease will return and stabilize. Satan can do this; he is the master of deception. I will not be deceived like this again.

Father, I take each thought captive and reflect on my wellbeing so as not to allow the evil one to rob me of my health. I petition you in Jesus' name for full healing and restoration. I pray also against the spirit of insomnia in the name of Jesus. I ask you to place your angels around me as I sleep, to safeguard my mind.

Lord, stress is a great problem; it is not conducive to bringing peace or completeness of body and soul. I'm grateful, Jesus, that you bestow imagination, but to imagine only good and visualize healing. I'm conscious that healing is a slow process, particularly for me—extremely slow. Father God, sometimes your hand moves slowly, but many times you intervene in an instant. Healing faith within is lacking. Why is this, Lord?

> *You know that without faith, I can do nothing. You have a great faith in many areas, but you have a block where your own healing is concerned. The devil finds a weak spot and works havoc in your life. Fight it like a plague, and do not accept the lie of a liar. He is the father of lies. Be aware, my precious child. I want you to distinguish between voices.*

Lord, it is true that Satan masquerades as an angel of light. We all need our spiritual senses activated to enable us to hear you and to more clearly discern your still small voice.

You continually bless us, but Lord, I often fail to see the blessing. At times I see your hand at work, but at other times it appears absent. Even so, God, I trust in your integrity. My suffering has been immense. I'm hopeful that you will not allow suffering beyond what we can bear, as you promised in relation to temptation.

Nevertheless, I believe you would not break the vessel you created. As you said, the supreme use of suffering is to purify. So, if I do not grumble, but work to have a healthy attitude toward suffering, regardless of the source, I shall find blessings hidden in hardships and sufferings. I trust you in this, Jesus. Please help me to grasp all you teach. I comprehend that faith and attitudes are incredibly worthy issues for healing in our physical life. When on earth, you sent the twelve disciples out to preach the kingdom of God and heal the sick; as Luke says, "They set out and went from village to village, preaching the gospel and healing people everywhere" (Luke 9:6).

Have you ever asked for or desired a healing ministry?

Instructions

Whoever gives heed to instructions prospers, and blessed is he who trusts in the LORD. (Prov. 16:20)

Consider this verse and its application.

Lord Jesus, it seems to me that the things of the Spirit cannot be learned entirely by our intellect. As we are in tune with you, it is spiritually perceived through the instructions of the Holy Spirit as He speaks within our spirit. Thank you, Lord Jesus, for directing me to 1 John 2:27: "As for you, the anointing you received from him remains in you, and you do not need anyone to teach you. But as his anointing teaches you about all things and as that anointing is real, not counterfeit—just as it has taught you, remain in him."

In Ephesians, as I read today, Paul says: "I keep asking that the God of our Lord Jesus Christ, the glorious father, may give you the spirit of wisdom and revelation, so that you may know him better. I pray also that the eyes of your heart may be enlightened in order that you may know the hope to which he has called you, the riches of his glorious inheritance in the saints" (Eph. 1:17). Lord, I wish to gain the wisdom spoken of in this verse and to invite you to teach me as you promised in 1 John. I want to learn from you and identify with you better.

> *My child, you do well to ask for wisdom. King Solomon asked exactly that. You will receive wisdom when you conquer the lessons I have been teaching.*

Thank you for your promise! Your Holy Spirit is a great teacher, but I am a poor pupil. Your lessons are not easy at times, Lord, but you teach so patiently. Jesus, I do appreciate the great privilege it is to be taught by you.

> *My lessons are easy or hard depending on your attitude toward them. My child, I watch over you. You take the time to serve me, and that delights me.*

Jesus, you have told me I am to teach, but James said, "Not many of you should presume to be teachers, my brothers, because you know that we who teach will be judged more strictly" (James 3:1). O my Jesus, it's a big responsibility—I wish not to lead any astray. Lord, I pray I may have insight and be true to your Word. Thank you, Jesus, for the Word you gave both my prayer partner and me.

I chose you, my daughters, for a special training I've given to only a few throughout the land. This does not mean that you two are spiritual giants—there are many who are more knowledgeable of the Word than are you. It is that I chose to do this through you both. Do not go out under your own strength; wait until I have given you specific guidance to do so. I need to prepare people, as all are at different stages in their spiritual growth. If you go ahead of me you could harden their hearts instead of drawing them to me—can you understand this?

Someday, all who look to me and are fully teachable will be led in the same way. But until then be obedient, listen to my voice, look to me, and rest in me. Be ready at my command to do my bidding, whenever I require you to, not whenever you aspire to. It may be too late or too soon. I have a perfect time for everything—every single thing. Think on these matters. Be ready, daughters, to make sacrifices for me! Each time I instruct you to go to or witness to a person, I have that person prepared. Can you see how important it is for you both to be so ready at all times? Bless you, my dear daughters.

Jesus, I aim to follow your instructions. It is by grace that I've been saved. Your leadership and guidance lead me to realize this in my innermost being. Frequently I felt everyone was worthier than me, but I see now that this was an inferiority complex—the other side of the coin to pride! It is an abomination to you, Lord, as pride too is focused on self and stems from self. It is the selfsame sin that Satan committed. Pride is a stronghold that is almost impossible to remove—unless you come to our aid, Jesus. It is essential to mature and follow your instructions no matter the inconvenience, no matter the complexity. In this way, Lord, I pray I can learn the lessons you teach so as to continue along the upward path of obedience to spiritual conquest.

My child, you must follow closely to what I tell you to do. The evil one will try to prevent you, but I will not allow him to tempt you beyond what you can bear. I permit circumstances to teach you to bring you to maturity. When you have despaired of all else and look to me, completely broken and humbled, I can use you. You will become a pure channel by looking to me and seeing me as I am in my humility, my majesty, and my might. Do not despair; I know you have been praying and waiting. Continue in this way, and I will say more to you about the way of guidance, my wonder child!

Jesus, you said in John, "I have much more to say to you, more than you can now bear. But when he, the Spirit of truth, comes, he will guide you into all truth" (John 16:12–13). The Holy Spirit is the most excellent teacher, my Lord. I choose to trust you and obey your instructions, which help to overcome all adverse circumstances, even the flesh that fights against the Spirit. The flesh dies hard but I will be victorious, as the evil spirits are ineffectual against the power of God, the Creator of the universe. I pray for my children. I pray I lead them in your ways, as there is no better way. I pray all your children will seek you for guidance. I thank you, too, for the wise instructions within your Word on child development and training.

Fathers, do not exasperate your children; instead, bring them up in the training and instruction of the Lord. (Eph. 6:4)

Read the instructive verses for nurturing children in Proverbs (Proverbs 1:8, 5:1, and 29:15 are a good start.) It doesn't matter whether you have children; the wisdom is to pass it on. Write down any highlights you uncover from this effort.

_____
_____
_____
_____
_____
_____
_____
_____
_____
_____
_____
_____
_____
_____
_____
_____
_____
_____
_____
_____

Overcoming Self

In this world you will have trouble. But take heart! I have overcome the world. (*John 16:33*)

Please examine this verse, thank Jesus, and seek him for assistance in overcoming the self-life within.

Lord Jesus, it's splendid that you take an interest in the insignificant, the grave, and the horrendous, as well as the most momentous and magnificent periods in our lives. No problem is too diminutive, nor is anything too colossal for you to turn to good. You give us the power to overcome: to overcome temptation and, most importantly, overcome the self-life within. You are all-sufficient. I believe it is your purpose to allow turmoil to touch our lives. I'm sure, Jesus, if only pleasant things were experienced, we would become indifferent and shallow, without understanding or compassion toward others. There is a need for balance, Lord. I believe we obtain this through both trials and blessings.

My Jesus, I do so thank you for the guidance you give in and through your Holy Spirit! I ask for your assistance to live out your instructions and apply them to my life. It's amazing how you place a book, a person, a sermon, or a Christian program in my path to reinforce the lessons you teach.

> *My child, you are more to me than you can possibly imagine. I go before you, leading and guiding you through the day. Do not hinder my work by your doubts and self-examinations. I know what you can do, and it is far greater than you yourself can imagine.*

I thank you, Jesus. You are the humblest person in the universe. I just marvel at your humility. There is so much pride in this world, although barely admitted as such. I pray that you would clear all doubts from my mind. I need help! You have taught me that it's impossible to earn my position in you, Christ Jesus. You gained that for me on the cross. You've taught about humility, to be humble toward you; humility is so essential in your kingdom. I've been striving to overcome self, yet the flesh, the old nature surfaces, unwilling to die. Its nasty head keeps popping up, demanding recognition. Oh, my Lord, I truly need support!

> *My child, don't forget the work is mine. I need an empty, clean, and teachable*

> *vessel in which to do my work. Relax, and allow me to work in you. Don't kick against the pricks.*

Lord, I'm at a loss to comprehend what you mean by "kick against the pricks" here, but I will relax. You say to let go of the self within; when this is achieved, then a powerful faith can bring forth innumerable victories.

> *My daughter, listen carefully to my instructions and overcome any impediment within. Obey me implicitly and all will be well. My timing is perfect. You do not know what awaits you, but be patient and trust me. I know what I am doing. I need to train you and discipline you, as I have a great work for you. Remember Peter: he failed me, but he was much used by me. So it is with you.*

Father God, I wish to "let go and let God," and to claim this Spirit guidance in overcoming the self-life.

> *I will lead and guide you; only give me the moments. This is a hard lesson to learn, but you are learning gradually. Keep up your endeavors, but at the same time rest completely in me. Know that I know all and can do all. I am your Lord and Master.*

Glory, Lord. How great you are, the source of light. As I overcome and die to this self-life within, your light and glory should shine more brightly, Jesus; I seem to fail and fail again when I attempt to shine a light for you. Jesus, how silly am I? I must be dead to self for this light to eventually shine; it has nothing to do with my attempts.

But no matter what our walk in life, others have walked it before, so I need not fear or strive in my own strength.

Prayer is humbling work. It abases intellect and pride, (and) crucifies vainglory.[12]

Prayer aids in overcoming the self-life; it reverses the blemishes within and builds character. Add praises to your Savior.

Our Source, Our Sacrifice

The Word was the source of life, and this life brought light to people. (John 1:4, GNT)

Does this verse speak deeply into your heart?

You, Lord Jesus, are the source of all that is ours. You provide the air we breathe, the water we drink, the life we live; you are the Creator of all things. Moreover, you are our sacrifice. You died so we may live.

Father God, I've been pondering the reason your son Jesus came to earth. As I've discovered, the Old Testament Law was unable to deal with the sinful nature. No earthly beings could be considered righteous or pure enough to be accepted as a sacrifice; we are all sinners, and the wages of sin is death. A spirit is not flesh and blood. Jesus, the Son of God, had to be born a flesh-and-blood human to represent us. The blood of lambs offered by the priests in the temple did not take away sin; it only covered it, and only for one year.

Almighty God, I thank you for the gift of your sinless Son Jesus Christ, the only unblemished person in the universe who could take our place and become the sacrificial lamb. By your sacrifice Jesus, our sins are removed and all who believe in you gain redemption. I fail to begin to understand how people can live in this sordid world without you, Lord Jesus. I praise you, Heavenly Father, for Jesus your only Son, who came and shed his blood for all mankind. He sacrificed all, he cleansed our conscience, and did away with our sins once and for all—washed them completely away, wiped them out. He destroyed the works of the serpent Satan—and I praise you, Lord, that the evil one has been defanged! Our enemy is now impotent and ineffective. Dear Father, I see that Jesus our Messiah came to live with us to teach us how to live with you.

At your second coming, Jesus, I look forward to your rule and to the time when Satan is thrown into the pit for the duration of the millennium. How glorious will it be to live under a leader who rules with love, integrity, and justice I assume not experienced in this world since the original sin. Without the temptations of Satan, it will be as at the beginning of time—paradise! Magnificent!

O Jesus, it's unbelievable: I read that after Satan's temporary release from the pit at the end of the millennium, many people will of their own free will follow him. How terribly sad for these poor deluded people; they follow him into the eternal lake of fire. Lord I pray those on my prayer list will not join that group. I trust that after the judgment, the folk who are left will go either into heaven or the new earth throughout eternity. Hallelujah, Jesus!

Heavenly Father, we humans all depend on you for life. You are the only source of life for all living things: humans, animals, birds, fish, and plants. Although there are some who do not realize it or want to admit it, you alone possess life and can give life. Father God, we humans are dependent upon you for our very existence, our very life, for every breath we take and for every move we make. Lord, it is the life within every living being that has great value in your eyes.

My mind boggles at your greatness. You are involved in this world in a greater way than I previously realized. There is not a thing you are unaware of, not a thought the billions of people who have lived, now live, and will live that you do not know, nor a motive of which you are ignorant. It must grieve you when so many people fail to recognize you. I pray they will give thanks to you for all you have provided, even their lives.

I am so grateful, Heavenly Father, that when Jesus returned to heaven, you sent us another, the Comforter, the Holy Spirit, who is the Spirit of truth. He it is who convicts us of sin and teaches and guides us into all righteousness. Lord, you do appreciate the sacrifice of our time and our money toward your purposes, but no matter the sacrifice we make, we will never enter your kingdom by our own effort, will we? Only the sacrifice you made, Jesus, could be sufficient to account for and pay the price for our transgressions.

Jesus, I'm genuinely delighted that you made me a new creation when I was born again, righteous and beautiful in your sight. It's distressing when people who are not born again but say they are Christians perform appalling deeds, bringing shame on your name and discrediting true Christians. But we must continue to look to you, stand firm, and endure to the end.

Lord, I'm grateful for the Holy Spirit's instructions. But who can fathom an iota of your intellect? It will take eternity to know of all your multifaceted divine character. You are incomprehensible and incommensurable—even in eternity I am unsure we will ever entirely comprehend your greatness. I believe we will still be discovering new aspects of your being throughout perpetuity. I fail to find a word to accurately describe your incomparability and preeminence. You are unquestionably the source of life and the source of all good.

> *Child, you do well to ponder my words. Leave all to me. The anointing you received remains in you. So be still and listen to that quiet, still voice, and you will know as you are known.*

Jesus, I believe you are the source of all knowledge. Knowledge is not found in the wisdom of the human race but only in you, Lord Jesus, through your Holy Spirit. There is so much that is needful to know. It appears to have taken me an eternity to learn. How much longer, Lord?

> *When you have learned the lessons I am teaching, to continue on the upward path toward me and my glory. Don't be despondent and think you are doing nothing! At times you will have other work to do, but*

right now this is your all-important work. All I ask of you is faith, trust, and obedience, and to rest in me. There will be a heavy price to pay at times, but my dear daughter, I have a great blessing for you. I will reach out and bless many people through you!

Jesus, you are truly our Source and our Sacrifice.

[Christ] has appeared once for all at the end of the ages to do away with sin by the sacrifice of himself. (Heb. 9:26)

Jesus is beyond doubt the source of our new life and redemption.

Why are attitudes important, and what is your attitude toward Jesus' sacrifice?

One Look at You

In simplicity, you made it so easy to come to you, Jesus!

One faithful look toward you is effortless and all it takes.

How would you describe your faith? Do you remember your first introduction to Jesus? Reminisce on this great experience.

Jesus, it is true that even a tiny child can call upon your name in faith and learn from you. You see our hearts, know our motives, and judge the sincerity of our repentance. Our salvation is a gift from you, Jesus. No matter the effort we make, it is impossible to earn this place by our works. Your Word says in Isaiah 64:6: "All our righteous acts are like filthy rags." O Jesus, we have many "do-gooders" in this world; these words must be hard for them to digest.

How effortless it is to be born again as spiritual babes, but the maturing and growing into Christlikeness is less so. As I see it, Heavenly Father, the discipline and training it takes to mature is not easily endured, but the results are heavenly.

Without your Holy Spirit within we can do nothing of eternal worth. Your training leads us to obey you, to overcome sin within, and to live lives that are pleasing to you, Lord Jesus. It is true that one look at you is all it takes. Your desire for us is to look to you; listen to your still, small voice; benefit from your wisdom; and encourage others. Being a Christian is certainly not trouble-free, but I pray, Jesus, in your name for the mental fortitude to humble myself under your training and thus become more Christlike.

My child, come aside and sit a while with me. Meditate upon all I have taught you. Your task is to teach others; to put me first, to take up their cross and follow me into the unknown—unknown to you, but not to me. Do not be afraid my dear one; I am with you.

Lord, I've been pondering holiness for some time. Later I read a word in *Come Away My Beloved* about that topic: "Holiness is not a feeling—it is the end product of obedience. Purity is not a gift—it is the result of repentance and serious pursuit of God."[13] I'm aware too, Lord, that suppression of self is key to godliness. Work that is performed in the flesh is what you would call "filthy rags." Jesus, I believe to be like you in obedience engenders holiness. Looking to you and desiring your presence is the answer.

Lord, I honestly need wisdom. You taught me that even spiritual ambition can stem from self, activated by pride. I clearly need your help!

> *My child, I have given you wisdom—not the wisdom of the world, but a measure of my wisdom. I want you to use it in all your decisions, and you will not veer far from my will. This will bring you the peace you pray for and the joy you receive from living close to and looking to me. You are being led along the road I mapped out for you from the foundation of the world. Be strong in me, and I will protect you from all evil. You are to go along, trusting me. I know what I am doing! I have a good purpose. You cannot see it, but I am in control!*

Lord Jesus, it's great to be led by you. I sometimes find it difficult to find my way around the blueprint planned specially for me. Nonetheless I give thanks to you that I am traveling in the right direction as you lead. You say, Jesus, that you know what you are doing. Often, I'm at a loss to know what you are doing, but as you say, keep looking to you and trusting you, as you know the way. This gives a feeling of complete security. I need not worry about anything, just relax in you.

Jesus, believers of the past, many who have since gone on to be with you, have greatly benefited today's Christians. I realize that in some cases I've looked to others too much in regard to spiritual matters instead of seeking you for guidance. It is essential now to continuously seek and directly go to you for direction. I'm grateful that you have given guidance and instructed me spiritually, and for that reason I sincerely thank you and glorify you. I wish to express my gratitude for your demonstration of how to live life as you intended when you created mankind and put them upon this earth. I dearly pray I will not bring shame upon your glorious name. O help me, Lord!

Continue to look to God, and keep your vision continually upon the Almighty; obey his instructions and pass them on.

Scrutinize the above statement and express your view on it.

_____
_____
_____
_____
_____
_____
_____
_____
_____
_____
_____
_____
_____
_____
_____
_____

Obedience

Take to heart all the words I have solemnly declared to you this day, so that you may command your children to obey carefully all the words of this law. (Deut. 32:46)

Praise God for one of his most precious gifts—little children.

Heavenly Father, my deep desire is to obey you and teach my children your ways. I wish to make a difference to society and create an everlasting impact worldwide—to influence as many as possible to seek after you. But without your help, this is an impossibility and cannot be achieved.

My child, I prepared the way for you. Walk in it, listen to me, and I will speak words of wisdom into your heart. I would have you travel the road mapped out for you, so be obedient to my leading. Be still and listen to my voice. In this way, you will always be in my will and you will never falter.

O my dear Jesus, never falter! I do at times falter but I'm conscious that when we don't listen to you, we miss your guidance. We need to be in the center of your will, that secret place with you. I sense we get there by complete obedience to the impressions, urgings, and promptings of the Holy Spirit within. Whenever we disobey, our spiritual growth is hindered. Much in this world is tempting, but failure to obey you and becoming tangled up in worldly affairs can sometimes bring dire consequences. This can take our eyes off you and place them onto much that is insignificant.

Child, do not do as many, who close their ears and follow the desires of their own hearts, then fall into the evil one's trap, which only leads to destruction. Let go of self and live only for me, your most loving Friend.

Father, I believe obedience to be paramount, to obey you, to surrender all, to allow your will to override my will, as I yield to your Holy Spirit, I pray he will help and empower me to love and obey you implicitly. Thus, become a suitable bride of Christ, as is your eternal purpose. Compliance is the secret, an additional key that allows entrance into your power, joy, and glory.

Lord, I recall years ago you warned me against attending our local church youth camp as it was not your will and outside the blueprint. Sadly, I convinced myself it was Satan speaking—I'd put much into this camp; three young attendees from our youth club were to be baptized; it was unimaginable that you would deny me! I convinced myself that it was paramount I be there. Once I arrived, specific situations made it abundantly clear that this was not where you wanted me to be. Jesus, as this truth struck me, I fell into remorse. It genuinely saddens me, Lord—the first and as has happened the last time I'd literally heard such a clear, audible voice, so forceful and so incredibly clear, and I disobeyed. I struggled against your will, but there was no excuse. Your voice was so authoritative that I should have been more discerning. I should have known, I should have realized, I should have obeyed. I've grieved and regretted it ever since. I've learned valuable lessons: Do not take God's word lightly. Do not fear what people think. Also, I learned that I am not irreplaceable. Lord, there was no justification for this denial of your command.

In your goodness you forgave me then, and I've forgiven myself, but I find it difficult to forget. Time and time again I contemplated what momentous earth-shattering plan you may have had in mind and what I'd missed. I'm inclined to think that it was a test of obedience—a test I failed miserably. I sense, Lord, how I must disappoint you because of that repulsive word "disobedience."

My child, you know I love you. You can do nothing to lose that love. You have ears to hear and a desire to do what is good and to obey my leading. But you do not say all that I require you to say. You are not witnessing to people about me as you should. Blessed are all who do my will and praise me for all they do not understand, although this is hard for them. But you know what I want, and do it ably, my precious one.

I wish to do better. Thank you for forgiving and forgetting. You shut out remembrance of my disobedience, precious Lord Jesus. Disobedience is such a colossal hurdle to overcome! You are an understanding and forgiving God, one who is above reproach. How you put up with my prolonged drawn-out pace in learning I cannot fathom.

I must seek you and love you, because in loving you I'll aspire to obey you. I may at times be blind to your will and fail to understand your mind and commands. However, that time, I would say it was blatant defiance. I'm so sorry!

If anyone loves me, he will obey my teaching. My Father will love him, and we will come to him and make our home with him. (John 14:23)

How do these words affect your life? Record your reflections.

Blind

Leave them; they are blind guides.
If a blind man leads a blind man, both will fall into a pit.
(Matthew 15:14)

Please pray for anyone you are aware of who may be blind in this way.

You, Lord, said through *Jesus Calling*, "Thankfulness takes the sting out of adversity. That is why I have instructed you *to give thanks for everything*. There is an element of mystery in this transaction: You give me thanks (regardless of your feelings), and I give you joy (regardless of your circumstance). This is a spiritual act of obedience—at times, blind obedience. To people who don't know me intimately, it can seem irrational and even impossible to thank me for heartrending hardship. Nonetheless, those who obey me in this way are invariably blessed, although difficulties may remain."[14] Lord, this explains much. It is not stupidity to follow you blindly, but it may be to follow man, as it's easy to be led astray by human wisdom. Jesus, I'm practicing giving thanks. This is not at all easy when under suffering pain and dire circumstances; I would prefer to wallow in self-pity.

Lord, I see people who seem blessed abundantly in this world but possess little or no empathy or respect for others struggling in different areas. They seem blind to their needs. Ephesians states, "Having the understanding darkened, being alienated from the life of God through the ignorance that is in them, because of the blindness of their hearts" (Eph. 4:18, KJV). I guess we all need to experience similar situations before we can possess any real understanding of the anguish of others—just as the sufferings you, Jesus, experienced as you walked on this earth. This enabled you to empathize and understand personally the sufferings, trials, and tribulations of the human race.

> *Child, I treat each differently. My hand is heavily upon you. I want you to be obedient to me always, blind obedience. Sometimes it will be difficult, but always blessings will come. The more you are obedient, the more light you will get.*

I'm certain, Lord, that obedience and submission are not at all times straightforward, yet it's of the utmost importance.

> *Thank you, my daughter, for being submissive to me. If only all my children were obedient, how wonderful it would be! So many more people would be brought into the kingdom.*

Help me Jesus, my Lord and my God, to comply with your request to obey—even, as you say, blind obedience—even though it may be beyond my understanding. I read of you in Hebrews, "Son though he was, he learned obedience from what he suffered and, once made perfect, he became the source of eternal salvation for all who obey him" (Heb. 5:8–9). Jesus, you were not blind to your purpose on earth; you submitted to your Father's will. You were well aware why you had come, and that was to achieve redemption for all mankind. Heavenly Father, this verse in Hebrews mystifies me, as Jesus was perfect from the beginning of time and beyond. So why then did he need to learn obedience? Perhaps it was his human side, the flesh, where he had to learn obedience. But again, that does not explain 1 Peter 1:19, who called Him "a lamb without blemish or defect." I sense Jesus in fact was perfect in himself but had to taste sin to identify with sinners, so as to take our place. Jesus submitted to you, Heavenly Father, to the point of sweating drops of blood in the garden of Gethsemane when he wrestled with the ordeal before him—the cross the suffering, isolation, abandonment, and desolation. Father God, at the cross Jesus became acquainted with the degradation of sin, as the entire world's sin was laid upon him? I guess at this point he met the criteria. Lord, this verse in Hebrews still puzzles me.

My child, there is much for you to know. Do not be anxious; all will be made known to you at the right time. Keep holding onto me and you will be taught; hence you will be able to teach others.

Jesus, you are certainly the source of eternal salvation for those who believe in you. I would venture to say your suffering was greater than any the human race ever encountered.

I praise you, Heavenly Father, that down through the ages Jesus' suffering has enabled him to empathize with mankind—our, trials, sufferings, and the temptation to sin.

Lord Jesus, I trust you don't mind my reasoning this through with you, as you know all things. You are our great High Priest who intercedes for us and understands our suffering and frailty. Dear Jesus, "thank you" is not adequate. There are not sufficient words to express my gratitude for the work of the Trinity. I need to thank you again that you broke the power of our enemy, Satan.

Meanwhile, if you, Jesus, had to learn obedience, how much more should we all learn it? I pray we will continue to walk in complete obedience, submit to you, and trust you sufficiently to follow your instructions blindly if necessary. You are trustworthy, Jesus, so none should hesitate to exhibit absolute trust in you, as soldiers in the army simply trust their commanders although they are unable to see the wider picture. I ask you to help us all to conquer self and completely surrender in blind obedience. O my Lord, it is not always painless!

And even if our gospel is veiled, it is veiled to those who are perishing.

The god of this age has blinded the minds of unbelievers, so that they cannot see the light of the gospel of the glory of Christ, who is the image of God. (2 Cor. 4:3–4)

How should you pray in respect to this verse? Jot down your thoughts.

Relinquishment

Do not be stiff-necked, as your fathers were; submit to the LORD. (2 Chron. 30:8)

The haters of the Lord should have submitted themselves unto him: but their time should have endured forever. (Ps. 81:15, KJV)

These biblical people were not willing to relinquish all to God. What cost are you willing to pay to surrender all?

Lord, I perceive that relinquishment is another crucial key in spiritual development—to deny ourselves and not deter the work of the Holy Spirit. I wish to place myself unreservedly before you, to be used for the furtherance of your kingdom. A vital factor is to sacrifice our time, our resources, and definitely our comfort zones. My Lord, that certainly is challenging—I truly value my comfort zone. It's a tricky one, Lord!

Dear Jesus, on the way to our eternal home, I sense the path is not always rosy. In fact, your path sometimes seems alien. Truly one must have a measure of holiness, a cleansed and fit vessel for heaven. There is a cost. So, Jesus, my days are all yours, I relinquish them into your hands and surrender all. Selfishness and pride must be left at the foot of the cross. Lord, to conquer self is one of the hardest and most difficult things to do, but with you and I together there shall be success. Because, Heavenly Father, when I am weak, you are able.

The burden will be lighter once relinquishment is accomplished. That's my hope, Lord. Please test my motives.

Daughter, if you desire to meditate, meditate upon me, and you will achieve much more than you do by always being reflective about your own motives.

Lord Jesus, my obedience needs working on. One ought to trust and obey you without question or hesitation. What I mean, Lord, is first-time obedience, just as I attempted to teach my own children. Jesus, scores of times I've been reluctant to relinquish myself to you completely—afraid of what you will ask of me, like public speaking.

Child, remember that the work is not yours but mine. You forget that. Be an empty channel and allow me to use you. My precious child, let go, and let me do the work through you. I love you, and I wish for you the happiness that can only be found in a close relationship with me, your Lord. Do not resent this time of training. I am training you to help you overcome and to relinquish all to me.

Jesus, I've always been a people-pleaser, I've never liked to disappoint. But you are more important than any earthly being. It is you I must please; it's you who must have first place in my heart. Therefore, I must relinquish my tendency to please people, but instead seek to please you. Jesus, emulation is another key. I hold this desire in my heart to model myself on you, but my endeavors fall far short. Perhaps you are too far above all human efforts; maybe I'm reaching for the sky. I am indeed as an ant in contrast to you, Lord.

My child, concentrate on me. You need not be apprehensive. Rest in me, and I will comfort and bring you to the point of surrender without the struggle you go through by your own efforts. You're slow to learn, you hold onto things and don't let go; you know what I mean. I can use you only as you relinquish all to me. Go now and do the duties I laid before you—you may find no excitement in them, but do them as my will for you, to glorify me. I will open doors as you come to them, and I will close those which you attempt to go through on your own.

Jesus, you said I know what you mean but I don't. I'm sorry; I see your frustration, but I do thank you, Lord, for your reprimands as they bring me back to the narrow path. Precious Jesus, I wish to be immersed in your love, relinquishing much of what I hold dear without complaint. Once selfish desires are dead, surrendered, and yielded up to you, and the self-life also dead, it's like a seed before it is planted in the ground. It's useless, but once planted and watered, it begins to germinate; then subsequently with your sunlight, it grows and multiplies and develops into a useful commodity. Lord, as I relinquish self and all is forfeited, I praise you for your assurance that this vessel too will become useful to you for the continual growth of your kingdom here on earth. Praise is important to you, Lord God. Praising you and looking to you brings you into our lives to do what we are unable to do. I praise you for the work you do in and through all your children when all is relinquished and surrendered into your hand.

Relinquishment is to surrender all. Do you find relinquishment difficult? What are some things in your life you find difficult to surrender? Enter your ideas here.

Reassurance

[S]ince we have a great High Priest over the house of God, let us draw near to God with a sincere heart in full assurance of faith. (Heb. 10:21–22)

Grasp this verse to your heart and say a silent prayer, thanking God for his reassurance.

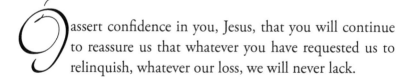

I assert confidence in you, Jesus, that you will continue to reassure us that whatever you have requested us to relinquish, whatever our loss, we will never lack.

My dear child, you are right to surrender all to me, to allow me to work in you to bring about the plan I ordained for you. Simply rest and relax in me, and don't be so introspective.

As I enlighten you, you will see more clearly. Bless you, my child.

Dear Jesus, I should not be afraid to relinquish whatever you require, even my desires! You say to let go of all worldly things and genuinely give up the joys and ways of this world for the far greater love of you. This does not result in loss but the assurance of all that you encompass. Lord, I attempt to do all to come to you totally surrendered, but unfortunately my human nature rebels!

My child, I want you to know I love you, and I don't find fault with you or judge you. I want to encourage you always to walk in my ways. As you relinquish all of yourself and all your desires and become one with me, I am able to work within you to accomplish my desire for your life. My precious child, relax in me, your loving Friend. I love you with all my heart; be assured of this promise. You are truly my joy, and I rejoice in you continually. Please rejoice in me, my beloved child.

Lord Jesus, you do not ask anything but that will benefit our souls; you are constantly reassuring me of your love. Thank you. The love you shower down upon me compensates for any lack.

My child, I tell you: You are to be blessed above and beyond all you can imagine. Be assured this is a time of self-surrender. Surrender all to me, your Lord and your Friend.

Lord, as I read back on what's written to you in my prayer journal over the years, I see countless I's. It's about you Jesus, not me! Lord, I fail to always keep my focus on you instead of self.

My child, as you surrender to me and relinquish all into my hands, your thoughts and your focus will become more centered on me and others—and therefore less on yourself. Your ministry at present is yourself; once conquered, you will be free for me to use as I wish and desire. You are pleasing to me, as I have told you. All go through a time of self-examination and struggle to come out of Satan's grip. You are at present in the stage of having the strands loosened that tie you to this earth. Rejoice in this, my child. I watch over you and see the progress you have made, and I too rejoice over you, my precious one.

Assurance of your love, Jesus, consoles me. I am so undeserving! I do wish to surrender all this world has to offer, and truly there is not much I hold dear. I pray all will gradually fade as these strands are severed. I express my gratitude for your reassurance. I give you first place in my heart. You surely are our

Exalted Lord! Please help me, Jesus, as I pray for others who also find this a battle against the evil one.

> *My child, man has complicated much; it is not the way I planned life on this earth to be. This is a fallen world, but I am working ceaselessly to bring as many into my kingdom as will come. I will not force anyone against their will, but certain folk are too busy even to stop and listen to my still, small voice within. I mourn for them, wait for them, and love them, but if they do not have a heart for me, I will not coerce them. The evil one will deceive and use all his evil power to drag them into hell, but that is not my way. I love you, my child.*

Jesus, your way has at all times been the way of love. In this age of grace, you encourage and reassure everyone of your love, believers and unbelievers alike. Jesus, I've figured out that their immoral, corrupt lives or perverted thoughts are immaterial to you. I'm not saying that you approve of evil undertakings, but you are so ready to pardon. Father, if these people would look to you and show genuine repentance, they would receive the assurance of your love. They would discover their lives changed and the desires of their hearts revolutionized. This guarantee of forgiveness and assurance of salvation would save them from the fiery pit. Jesus, I pray in your name they will look up to you and surrender all. The most powerful love that fills the human heart with joy is your promise for all your created ones. This is such inspiring news. Jesus, you are the God of all comfort. I appreciate you, for in you we are enriched in every way. Thank you, Jesus.

But continue thou in the things which thou hast learned and hast been assured of, knowing of whom thou hast learned them.
(2 Tim. 3:14, KJV)

Has your life been enriched? Do you have assurance within your heart of this enrichment? Share about it below.

36

Thoughts

For the word of God is living and active. Sharper than any double-edged sword,

it penetrates even to dividing soul and spirit, joints and marrow; it judges the thoughts and attitudes of the heart.
(Heb. 4:12)

Deliberate quietly on God's special Word.

Multiplicities of thoughts within my mind wander around the world. O my Lord Jesus, I require assistance to control my thoughts and relinquish all selfish ones and focus only on you. Attempts to discipline my mind seem insurmountable. Lord, I do so much have need of you. Negative thoughts crowd in, and criticisms destroy inner tranquility. With determination I endeavor to guard against hurtful words, which always begin as thoughts—words can be withdrawn before spoken, but emphatically not afterward! Lord, even as I write this, I realize I must not continue to ask for help in controlling my thoughts but instead ask that your thoughts be my thoughts. Today, Jesus, my thoughts are on you as I contemplate the greatness of your love.

The most momentous occasion for mankind, Heavenly Father, was the incarnation, when you offered your Son Jesus, who relinquished all to die in our place although we were undeserving and covered in sin. You were not in the dark about our iniquitous ways and selfish thoughts. You simply loved us. I sense human nature today is no better than at Noah's time. My thoughts are, Lord: In this time of grace, why are we so blessed? By the power of your Holy Spirit, you work to transform each of us into the people you thought of and envisioned when you created us in the womb, bringing about your individual plan for each unique individual. I truly thank you for your blessings and kind thoughts toward me, although they're unmerited.

In Isaiah 55:9 you say, "As the heavens are higher than the earth, so are my ways higher than your ways and my thoughts than your thoughts." Clearly Lord, your divine thoughts are way beyond the understanding of my finite mind. The Bible speaks much of your love; you carried out your love in action with the redemption of mankind. My thoughts are, Lord, that if love is not carried out in action, then it is not reality. You say, "Take captive every thought to make it obedient to Christ" (2 Cor. 10:5). Father God, I believe that's what Jesus did in the garden of Gethsemane; he took his thoughts captive.

Jesus, lack of concentration is a problem to overcome when thoughts wander back and forth when reading the Bible or praying. It is difficult sometimes to distinguish whether these thoughts originate from Satan or from my own meandering thoughts.

> *Child, there is not a thing that I don't know about you, not a thought of yours that I am unaware of. You think that I don't come to you. However, I am with you every day, every moment; you are pleasing to me, but as you grow in maturity, you will learn more and more to trust me. Leave everything to me and trust me to take control. I see all and know all. Who else can you rely upon to work out your affairs? Who better than me, your Lord? I love you, and you hurt me when you do not completely trust me.*

O my Jesus, it is heartrending to realize that my doubts and negative thoughts grieve you! I'm so sorry. Please have pity on this mortal soul. I ask you, Lord, to change my heart so that sweet and loving thoughts come forth, and beyond all to grow in grace and live in purity and holiness. I praise you for the vitality, joy, and freedom I have in you, and realize it's imperative that I become more familiar with your will and learn to differentiate between the voices of good and evil. With your help, Lord, I desire to maintain control over negative thoughts and rise above judgmental views.

It is true that negative thoughts cause drastic effects. Anxious thoughts churn stomachs and bring about negative consequences such as an unbridled tongue and delayed healing. As thoughts are, so is the flesh. Devastated bodies and minds cause serious grief. My old nature struggles for supremacy; I wish the devil would go away. I wrestle with uncontrolled thoughts. Optimistic thoughts create tranquility and a healthier body, and all anxiety dissipates instantly. Protect, I pray, Jesus, my subconscious mind as I substitute positive thoughts for negative ones. Please take pity upon me, Lord Jesus; I feel so overwhelmed.

> *Focus always on me, your Savior. I am the only one who can save you from negative thoughts planted in your mind by the evil one. I love you. Wake up from your slumber and walk out into the sunlit glades with me, your Lord, your Friend, your Redeemer. My child, you are so precious to me. I love you dearly.*

I love you too, my Lord, my God. Please help me to love you more. Heavenly Father, you are our true Father throughout eternity, long past the days of our earthly fathers on this earth. My thoughts are on the billions of human beings, each created uniquely, not a soul fashioned alike. I marvel at your awe-inspiring creativity! But saying that—you are God!

Search me, O God, and know my heart; test me and know my anxious thoughts. (Ps. 139:23)

Have you ever asked God to shine his spotlight on your heart?

If so, what has been the outcome? I invite you to write the effect on your life below.

My Creator

For we are God's workmanship, created in Christ Jesus to do good works, which God prepared in advance for us to do. (Eph. 2:10)

Think about the works that God ordained for you before you were born. Have you discovered these? If not, seek him for the answer; he cares for you, and he will not hold any good thing from you.

Heavenly Father, as my thoughts linger on you today, I reflect and puzzle upon the fact that you have no beginning and no end. If some entity had created you and brought you into being, the question would be raised of how that being came to be, and so on it would go. Hence, you eternally existed. I likewise fail to comprehend how it is that the universe has no end—but it would be more puzzling to envisage if it did, as I would then question what was on the other side!

The more I contemplate these things, the more they mystify me. I suppose this is the natural complexity of thinking outside the box. Everything upon this earth has a beginning and an end. Once again, I wonder what it will be like to live in a timeless zone in heaven—this too is incomprehensible. Lord, music on earth beats to time—what does the heavenly music sound like in a timeless zone? I speculate, yet these call for patience; I expect they will be discovered when we arrive at our heavenly abode.

You simple amaze me, Lord God, the methods you use to teach and the way you worked in the Scriptures. The unusual bringing down of the Jericho walls, Jonah in the big fish, Daniel in the lion's den, the three young men in the fiery furnace, the resurrection of Lazarus from the grave and your miraculous healing powers. There is no limit to your creativity in demonstrating your power.

Almighty God, I reflect on you as the Creator of the universe and all that it contains. It bewilders me how evolutionists could suppose that the world and all it includes happened by chance—created itself out of nothing. They tell us it all evolved over millions of years through natural change, although from what I've read, they have yet to come up with an honest example of an intermediate species—never mind that if their theory is correct, there should be millions.

Lord, a design requires a designer; whatever is built requires a builder. You, Jesus, are both designer and builder and all with a purpose; nothing is by chance. How a mindless nonentity could create our intricate planetary systems and the laws that govern the universe, I do not know. It would require intelligence beyond man or any created being to plan and create this world and all living entities. To contemplate the complexities of an atom. . . . The simplest cell is incredibly complex. It's unrealistic to imagine that even a small thing such as an eye, with all the intricacy of detail involved in sight, was created out of nothing by nothing; I fail to fathom their reasoning. I sorrow for those who have invested a lifetime in a futile attempt to discover phenomena that is impossible to ascertain apart from you, the Creator.

I'm of the opinion, Lord, they are merely endeavoring to be comfortable in their unbelief. This is the problem, Jesus: they fail to recognize either you or your Word. Billions of dollars are spent endeavoring to work out how the universe began, and all people need to do is open the Bible, and the first verse would tell them.

Jesus, I pray to you, my Lord, that these people will accept you as the Creator and that you will become a living reality to them. You who created all things are able to perform powerful marvels as well as minute diminutive tasks. Human combined knowledge must barely be a minuscule percentage in contrast to yours! As Creator there is nothing impossible for you and nothing you do not know.

My desire is to pray in agreement with your will, which enables injustices to be addressed so that the world becomes a better place, kind and humane. You are not a silent God! You speak as you did in biblical times. It's not that you are silent, but that I am often deaf—as are, I would dare say, various other Christians. I pray you would aid me to still my thoughts and help me to hear your still, small voice more distinctly.

My child, sit quietly and meditate upon me. Still your thoughts and listen, and you will hear. This will take practice and perseverance on your part.

Jesus, I do find it difficult to still my thoughts. But I thank you, Almighty God, Lord and Creator for your help. "O Lord, our Lord, how majestic is your name in all the earth!" (Ps. 8:9). I praise you, my Lord, that you came to this earth to save us from the fate of our own wickedness.

For by him all things were created: things in heaven and on earth, visible and invisible, whether thrones or power or rulers or authorities; all things were created by him and for him. He is before all things, and in him all things hold together.
(Col. 1:16–17)

Various people experience doubt about this verse, about creation. What are your thoughts on this subject? Jot them down.

58

Christmas

*For to us a child is born, to us a son is given. . . .
And he will be called Wonderful Counselor, Mighty
God, Everlasting Father, Prince of Peace.
(Isa. 9:6)*

Does this bring joy to your heart? What glorious words to ponder!

It's enjoyable to share your birthday with you and my family Jesus—whatever the correct day may be! I know December twenty-fifth is likely not it, but I don't truly consider it be of significance. Some Christians don't celebrate Christmas; they say it's a pagan day. But Lord, had I lived back in those days I would have said, "Let's get together and celebrate Jesus' birthday instead of joining their pagan festival." It's easy to imagine that's what the early Christians did. Each day is a day for contemplation upon you, to celebrate and worship you. It's our inner thoughts, pure hearts, and our close fellowship with you that are central, I believe, not so much our activities.

As we approach this Christmas, Jesus, I meditate on that first morning when you came upon this earth. I imagine that midnight hour in the hush of the night, when the only sounds heard were the rejoicing voices of angels as they gave praise and glory to God in the Highest. I sit in silence and stillness and ponder the great love that brought you into this world so long ago. Happy birthday, Jesus!

Many countries celebrate Christmas, but frequently you are not invited. Even in my country, this day is a day to celebrate, but in various homes not with you. This must disappoint you. Your title, Christ, is often omitted in the word "Christmas" spelt as "Xmas." Lord, they have almost put you completely out of sight altogether: prayers discontinued in schools and attempts to do away with the ten commandants in the courts. My heart yearns for these ill-informed people. Jesus, you came with love to save those whose desire it is to eliminate you from society. I pray they will call to you and be saved from suffering throughout perpetuity.

I sit quietly and reflect upon you today. You left heaven, that glorious place, a place of purity, a place of splendor and glory, rich beyond description.

Incredible Jesus, although you are God, the King of the universe, yet you came to this sin-ridden planet to be born in a dirty, stinking stable, where wicked, jealous people determined to kill you, confronted you with lies, ridiculed you, and spat upon you. It's so unbelievable, people wanting to kill God—but that is exactly what happened. But this was only possible because of your will. Humans have no control over you. Jesus, you came at the Father's appointed time to save us from ourselves, as was your plan. You sacrificed yourself freely for all mankind when you died on the cross. Lord, they treat your people the Jews and Christians in similar ways today; many in certain countries wish to kill us.

Long eons ago, Father, before you sent your Son to be born as a babe in Bethlehem, this world was only a thought in your mind until you spoke and brought it into being. Your thoughts for your created ones were for good and not for evil, so all good things were available to us. Unfortunately, we used our free will to go our own way and spoiled our paradise.

Heavenly Father, your purpose for Jesus being born of a virgin, on that Christmas morning so long ago, was to take our sins and die in our place. I thank you, Jesus, for the exchange you made on the cross. You gave your life in exchange for our salvation. It was your life for our life. If you had not come, we would have been doomed in sin, without any possibility of redemption. But praise you, mighty Jesus, you humbled yourself and came in humility as a human on that first Christmas morning almost two thousand years ago. Now all is not lost; rather, all things are possible. Jesus, you died and rose again, resurrected from the grave in glory and great power. You are unquestionably the light of the world!

The people walking in darkness have seen a great light; on those living in the land of the shadow of death a light has dawned. (Isa. 9:2)

How does this verse speak into the depth of your heart?

Pride

Pride goes before destruction, a haughty spirit before a fall.
(Prov. 16:18)

Please read the book of Proverbs at your earliest convenience; it imparts much wisdom.

Jesus, you are so humble; you exhibit not an iota of pride. You are the majestic and exalted God who guides us to surmount and triumph over the inevitable obstacles of pride.

Lord, you bring us through periods of animosity; you help us work through wrong thought patterns, pride, and other shortcomings. Once these things are totally conquered, gradually a fuller awareness of your presence and endearing joy will come. I thank you for your assistance and your instructions.

My child, be patient. Although you do not always feel my presence, I am with you, loving you, caring for you, uplifting you, waiting for you, and watching to see you overcome those things that hinder your faith. Child, be aware I love you unconditionally. I know your weaknesses; I know your strengths. I allow only that which will bring about your ability to overcome and grow to maturity so I can use you for the most important work there is on this earth, and that is to grow into my likeness. I want you to come into my kingdom as a joyful, pure, and holy vessel.

Jesus, it's essential to overcome temptations. I so frequently fail in this endeavor! But whenever the thought comes to mind that I've made it, you let me know that you are unable to use me because of spiritual pride. I've been pondering the reason I fear failure. You said, "It's pride." And I'm sure that's correct; I worry because I don't wish to be perceived a failure. This has prevented many attempts at countless things, as I've doubted my ability to succeed.

My prayer, Jesus, is for undeserved favor to help overcome worry, doubt, and pride—all sins against you, Lord! They are purely the product of lack of faith in you and in myself. Since I met you that magnificent day, there has never been doubt of your being—only unworthiness that I should seek from you, Almighty God, that you would even notice me. I ask for forgiveness. Jesus, most future things that entangle our minds with worry and anxiety have already dissipated by the time we get to them. To worry implies a fear of failure and the future. Dear Lord, I pray to overcome the fear of failure and be victorious!

My dear, you have no need to even think of failure. I am with you, walking with you and watching over you in whatever task I set before you. Do not fear, my child! I am here to help you; you have only to call. Do not forget I am your Savior. You are my own, and I love you dearly. Do not think of yourself as less than others; just think of yourself as one who has been redeemed by the One who is no respecter of persons. Do not despair.

Jesus, failure is not always disastrous, as we can all learn by our mistakes. I guess that's the reason that you, at times, decide not to shield us from our blunders. You often emphasize the danger of pride and other inadequacies within our lives. You must grieve about our doubts and fears. I pray my shortcomings don't cause a drift in our relationship. Please, Lord, empower me to remedy these flaws and overcome pride. I wish to not be constantly seeking forgiveness.

My child, nothing will come between you and my love for you—not even your shortcomings, as you say. Child, please read Romans 8:35, 37-39.

Jesus, how great your love and forgiveness is! These are glorious verses! I'll type them out:

> Who shall separate us from the love of Christ? Shall trouble or hardship or persecution or famine or nakedness

or danger or sword? . . . No, in all these things we are more than conquerors through him who loved us. For I am convinced that neither death nor life, neither angels nor demons, neither the present nor the future, nor any powers, neither height or depth, nor anything else in all creation, will be able to separate us from the love of God that is in Christ Jesus our Lord.

Jesus, I should memorize these remarkable verses. Paul had boundless faith and appeared devoid of pride. To trust in your love and never doubt is the way. Definitely pride or an inferiority complex is a hindrance.

We need always to rejoice, Jesus, that our failures and shortcomings do not hinder our friendship! You are precise and unhurried, and you show bounteous amounts of patience. In comparison to many of us whose schedules are rushed and hectic, your timing is perfect. I think pride drives us; we often seem to be seeking to achieve and achieve, and for what? Much is pointless. We all need the fortitude to wait and listen for your commands, which enable us to discover your will. Only then will we seek the rewards of heaven; all else is futility.

Jesus, you have said on numerous occasions that nothing can be achieved by haste; you wish all to relax in you and live our daily lives in conjunction with the blueprint you mapped out for each of your children. Impatience does not glorify you; I'm learning that! An attempt to overcome this sin has been futile, but thankfully, all was forgiven when I accepted your sacrifice, that horrifying death on the cross. It is true, Jesus, our sins were forgiven when we repented, but we still often have to suffer the consequence. Thankfully, Lord, you walk with us through the effects of these sins, especially the sin of pride.

What a glorious world if all our aspirations were to grow like you in your humility, to impress you instead of attempting to impress others, and to live as you set the example while on earth. It is impossible to ever resemble you in my being—you are omnipotent, omniscient, and omnipresent. But to grow like you in character: loving, caring, tender, merciful, gentle, and humble, exhibiting all the fruit of the Spirit. Wow, what a magnificent life would that be!

> *Child, you compensate for the rejection I encountered while on earth. A great reward awaits you in heaven, my daughter. Please keep on the narrow path I have laid out for you.*

Jesus, you are our majestic and exalted God who works tirelessly for all your children—what an amazing phenomenon to comprehend! So, Jesus, along that narrow road I will triumph and surmount inevitable obstacles, including the great hurdle of self-importance. Lord, you relied on your Father when on earth; therefore, we too need our reliance to be upon you and ask for help in this issue of pride. Pride shows up as arrogance and egotism. How horrid. Pride does not come from you, Lord, but the devil.

For all that is in the world, the lust of the flesh, and the lust of the eyes, and the pride of life, is not of the Father, but is of the world. (1 John 2:16, KJV)

Pride is the sin of Satan, his war against God's people. What is your view on this matter?

Baptism of Fire

*He will baptize you with the Holy Spirit and with fire.
(Matt. 3:11)*

Who can endure the day of his coming? Who can stand when he appears?

For he will be like a refiner's fire. (Mal. 3:2)

What is your belief on the baptism of fire?

Lord, trials are as a fire but also a blessing. It's our reaction to them that is paramount. If we crumble under them, we have learned nothing. To embrace suffering positively is to gain the prize. Jesus, I know this in my head, but I'm sorry, it has yet to reach my heart.

Dear child, this is your challenge at present.

O my Lord, Jesus, in the beginning I was so in awe of you, I seemed almost afraid to approach you. In my ignorance, I asked you for the baptism of fire. Furthermore, I was oblivious to the cost and what it would entail—the pain, trauma, anguish, and hardship. Consequently, I figured out that the Christian road was not all rosy. Many times, I've regretted asking for the refiner's fire. Nevertheless, I cannot request you quench it until your purpose has been obtained—until the dross has been burned out and my life is as pure as gold. Wow!

I read in *God Calling*, "Between my promise of the gift of Joy to my disciples and their realization of that Joy came a sense of failure, disappointment, denial, desertion, hopelessness, then hope, waiting, and courage in the face of danger. Joy is the reward of patiently seeing me in the dull dark days, of trusting when you cannot see."[15] Jesus, I'm fully aware that all go through hardships and trials, but I pray to conquer with absolute reliance on you. It is unwise to focus on problems or sufferings, as this takes our eyes off you, the One who can walk us through the fiery furnace to freedom and victory.

Again Lord, in *God Calling* you said: "All that depresses you, all that you fear are powerless to harm you. They are but phantoms. The real forces I conquered in the wilderness, the Garden of Gethsemane, on the Cross, in the Tomb."[16] Jesus, these "forces" do appear real to me at the present moment. But I thank you, Lord—you overcame all for us, even death. No matter the strife I've to battle through, it is true; joy comes in the morning—may not be the next morning or the next, but it does come. With you, dear Jesus, I believe victory is assured; it's the timing I struggle with. Patience is lacking.

Jesus, my favorite leisure time is reading biographies and autobiographies of godly people who you used mightily. Time and again I noticed that they too had gone through multiple trials, and some the baptism of fire. Following you is not trouble-free, is it? Lord Jesus, I've learned from these godly men and women. I learned that life's sufferings and fiery trials do not hamper our development but help us along the road to conquest. But Lord, it's been a taxing time; it's not easy to rejoice in afflictions. Repeatedly I've thought this season cruel and callous; it has truly been a baptism of fire.

My child, I do experience the suffering you're going through. I go through it with you. Yes, your sufferings have been necessary for the work ahead, but always remember that when my children suffer, I suffer too. Just remember that I am with you. I will always be beside you, and underneath are my everlasting arms.

In *Jesus Calling,* you said, "Every problem can teach you something, transforming you little by little into the masterpiece I created you to be. The very same problem can become a stumbling block over which you fall, if you react with distrust and defiance. The choice is up to you, and you will have to choose many times each day whether to trust me or defy me."[17]

I must apologize, Lord, for the time it has taken for me to get to the point where a measure of your image of me becomes a reality. Going through the baptism of fire is all-consuming. Your disciples of old, too, shared in your sufferings and the fiery trials. We as your followers cannot ask for any reduction. I imagine the travail of soul you have suffered since your resurrection as you await your people's repentance and surrender. I would say we've delayed your coming in power and great glory ever so much. But even as I say that, I know you have a timetable. Since you see the future, I imagine that timetable is fixed. But then, perhaps you can change your mind.

John answered them all, "I baptize you with water. But one more powerful than I will come, the throngs of whose sandals I am not worthy to untie. He will baptize you with the Holy Spirit and with fire." (Luke 3:16)

What great challenge do you see in this verse?

41

Storms

I would hurry to my place of shelter, far from the tempest and storm. (Ps. 55:8)

Do you have a safe haven from the storms in your life? Are you a safe haven for friends who may at times need a refuge?

Life storms are a great battle—and a losing one unless you, Jesus, come to our aid! I know you are the controller of storms, not only of the weather but of the storms that ravage our inner lives. You gave your people the full armor of God to stand against the devil and his hordes and the authority to deal with and triumph over them in your name, Jesus. The greatest thing is to praise—the devil cannot stand against praising Christians.

Lord, we need to accept the fact that in life we will encounter many trials and raging storms. We should resolve to overcome these in your power, and as you walk with us through them, we cannot fail. How people go through this earthly life without you, Jesus, I know not.

I do pray for those in my country who have lost loved ones during the ferocity of these latest storms, and the many who have survived but whose homes the tempests have left uninhabitable. I ask that you will be close to them and pray they will call to you in their distress and be supported and comforted. I ask a blessing too, Jesus, upon the compassionate people who have supported them so generously and selflessly. I understand their hardship, Lord Jesus. While under trials and tribulations, my life has seemed precariously fragile. Sporadically I sense I'm drowning in stormy waters when I encounter sufferings and all manner of trials and various tests.

> *My child, you stand in gale-force winds in the storm and rain. You have allowed those storms to weather your face for me. You haven't worried. You have stood the test of time. You have stood through storms, stood through fierce winds and the harsh beating rains of adversity; you have allowed me to become everything to you.*

Praise you, Jesus, the literal storms and floods have ceased, but regrettably at present my heart aches for our country that seems to be ablaze with fire. Climate change is again blamed for this. I inquired previously, Jesus, it is you? You are in charge of nature, storms, and fire too, as we see the three men in the furnace. Again, Jesus, your prophecies in Luke 21:25–26 state the perplexities that will occur at the end of this age. I'm sure you are sending a wake-up call by showing your power in nature, to cause us to be ready as you are returning soon. I appeal to you, Jesus, to comfort the people who have lost loved ones and homes—those who are caught up in these horrendous fires that storm through, wiping out properties and food supplies. I pray they will encounter your nearness and call to you for comfort.

Lord, I do hold onto the verse in Philippians that says, "I can do everything through him who gives me strength" (Phil. 4:13). You also bring good out of what can be viewed as undesirable experiences; nothing is wasted. I pray that many will see your hand in this and know that you are God who is all-powerful. By faith I give you thanks for the pressure periods, the storms, and the harsh times, just as I do the good times. And Lord, I genuinely thank you that there have been bounteous good times.

Jesus, in Revelation you tell us that we are to overcome; consequently, there must be multitudes of different storms to take place and wade through and conquer. I guess, Lord, we need these massive tests to build courage to navigate the rocky roads where you lead us on occasion. I pray for patience in the face of trouble and for the perseverance that builds character. Lord, it is true: the Holy Spirit cannot be quenched without suffering grief. Only in retrospect can the purpose behind our anguish be seen. I glorify you and give thanks that everything—even the threats, intimidations, abuse, and maltreatment—has been worked together for good.

> *I love you, my daughter. This is a training experience for you. I have great things ahead for you, so your training must include*

> *an exhaustive regime. You are not alone; I am beside you, walking with you. And I do appreciate the suffering you are willing to go through for me. My love is so great for you that I almost want to save you from the hurt you feel, but this road is necessary for your purification and strength.*

Lord, I do believe you would spare all if you did not love so—instead, you work for our best interest, for the betterment of our souls. Slowly I am learning to grasp the concept that this is the way of conquest. Lord Jesus, you are the great shield against the consequences of our faults, failings, and weaknesses. I pray for more faith to rise up as an eagle and soar above these mountains of difficulty, and climb to greater heights to escape the fiery darts of the evil one. Paul said to Timothy, "Endure hardship with us like a good soldier of Jesus Christ" (2 Tim. 2:3). Once more Paul said, "I consider that our present sufferings are not worth comparing with the glory that will be revealed in us" (Rom. 8:18).

Precious Jesus, amidst the joys of life, you are here, and through the storms of life, you are here. You comfort me, O Lord. These stormy trials in life are ultimately the way to our destiny! We all wade through storms, Lord. I pray you will not allow these storms to conquer us, nor permit them to impede our progress, but that you will enable us to master them. As it is said, "The men of Judah were victorious because they relied on the Lord, the God of their Fathers" (2 Chron. 13:18). Father God, I pray all who read this book will endeavor to rely on you likewise, and that as you walk with them, there is no doubt victory will be assured.

Please renew our efforts and keep us on the narrow road that leads to the heavenly kingdom. Honestly, we are all in need of you, Jesus.

> *My precious, precious child, I am there with you when you need me. I am there as you go through the valley. You think your suffering is something terrible that you must endure alone; but remember I am with you, and I will show you a way out. I lead you through temptations and storms. I never leave you.*

It is true, my Lord, you never leave us alone. You are in control of the storms of life and also the weather, as can be seen in the shipwreck Paul endured on his way to stand trial before Caesar: "When neither sun nor stars appeared for many days and the storm continued raging, we finally gave up all hope of being saved" (Acts 27:20). Although the boat was wrecked, Paul and all lives on board were saved.

God is in control of the weather; climate change too is in his hands.

He knows what his is doing!

No matter the tragedies in life, you can obtain comfort knowing God is in control.

Write down your observations on this matter.

_____
_____
_____
_____
_____
_____
_____
_____
_____
_____
_____
_____
_____
_____
_____
_____
_____
_____

Nothing Alien

[T]here is nothing new under the sun. (Eccl. 1:9)

Do you sometimes have the impression that you deal with matters that appear alien? How does this affect you?

Lord Jesus, each person you created is unique—but is this true of circumstances within our lives? King Solomon told us that nothing is new. Lord, I can see that nothing is alien in the aspect that human nature has not changed since creation. We are still passing the buck and blaming each other. The first person born was a murderer, and murder has been a part of life down through the ages and is still committed today.

In relation to technology, mechanics, and flight, these and other countless inventions and discoveries would certainly be alien to our ancestors. King Solomon, after much of his negativity in Ecclesiastes, stated, "Fear God and keep his commandments" (Eccl. 12:13). Lord, that is not alien. That is the living word throughout all eternity.

Lord Jesus, should I be surprised at the painful trials in my life, as if something alien was occurring? These occurrences are not alien, even if they seem so to me! I appreciate and thank you that you will never leave us alone; although you have conveyed this several times, I still rejoice in this fact. Jesus, when I remind myself that I am on a journey to heaven, all the trials and tribulations diminish in the light of eternity. There is no reason to lose heart! As the apostle Paul said: "Though outwardly we are wasting away, yet inwardly we are being renewed day by day. For our light and momentary troubles are achieving for us an eternal glory that far outweighs them all. So we fix our eyes not on what is seen, but what is unseen. For what is seen is temporary, but what is unseen is eternal" (2 Cor. 4:16–18).

The psalmist said, "Be still, and know that I am God" (Ps. 46:10). Lord, stillness is quite alien in today's society. Yet no matter the circumstances and trials, I put my trust in you. I do not wish to be like the person described in James as "double-minded." Instead, I will "Consider it pure joy . . . whenever [I] face trials of many kinds" (James 1:2). Lord, this verse certainly seems alien.

Jesus, yesterday I heard it said that those who follow the Christian religion are weak and in need of a crutch. Lord, all of humanity is in need of you. You are the Almighty Son of God; without you we would all be doomed. On the contrary, Lord, we're not weak. We are empowered by you, the overwhelming, majestic God, to achieve monumental deeds and mighty miracles through your strength.

The true Christian life is not unproblematic; in fact, I'm sure no one can successfully live it without the power of the Holy Spirit! The demands to be joyful in the midst of trials and tribulations go far beyond our sinful nature to handle. So, Lord, these alien or assumed alien trials I encounter, whatever they may be, will invariably bring me out strengthened and empowered. To nonbelievers, I am sure the true Christian life is alien to them.

Satan is putting more and more panic, anxiety, and depression upon people these last years. I can see it and even feel it myself. Satan fires deceptive thoughts into our minds. Thanks to you, Lord Jesus, who won the victory over him, he has only whatever power we allow him. I rebuke each alien or negative thought planted in my mind by the evil one in Jesus' name, before they become established and entrenched.

Jesus, I hope to refrain from self-introspection, as it merely brings disappointment. Only praise will lift feelings of despair and sorrow. That's it, Lord, isn't it?

> *My child, I expel the darkness and heaviness in your heart. Do not fear, but trust; focus only on me. You ask constantly when this testing time will come to an end. When you do that, you focus on your trials and problems and not on me. Please, my child, do not continue in this way, as you hinder the very thing you pray for.*

I'm so repentant, Lord; please forgive me. After speaking to you yesterday for advice on the encounter with a certain business, I decided not to write to the CEO of the company with reference to unfair treatment. As you know, I intended to put my case before them but then relented. You are my avenger; my reliance must be upon you. It is you who will avenge. This situation is not strange or alien. We are not alone; all go through mistreatment of different kinds. So, as you say, dear Jesus, I'll "let go and let God."

> *My child, you don't need to defend yourself. It is I who will avenge, and it is I who defend the innocent. Don't be like the world. Let go of this, as in the light of eternity it is of no importance. As an earthly vessel, you see what took place as a great injustice. I see it as an opportunity for you to "let go and let God." Remember, my dear child, you can do all things through Christ who strengthens you. What I mean by that is that you can do all I ask of you as I enable you. Go now, my dear, and don't allow the things of the world to drag you down. I love you with an everlasting love.*

It is true you are undoubtedly my defender. Jesus, since I put this state of affairs into your hands, it has almost been wiped from my memory. What I once thought of as *a great injustice*, a mountain, is now not even a molehill. Your words help me recall that I must constantly judge the value of everything by whether it leads to you and to heaven. And Jesus, that is not alien—that is well known. Lord, you do defend your people. In this I give you thanks.

Lord Jesus, I know there is no reason to fear. You are near to me, but I'm aware only in the present. You give us merely twenty-four hours to live in. The past is behind; the future is yet to come. I know, Lord, that only a tiny fraction of worries ever come to fruition, so it is daft to agonize about the future. I leave the future in your hands and I trust you, Lord, to prepare the way for all who believe to that idyllic place—heaven!

[A]t that time ye were without Christ, being aliens from the commonwealth of Israel, and strangers from the covenants of the promise, having no hope, and without God in the world.
(Eph. 2:12, KJV)

Say a prayer for those who are without Christ, that they may join us in heaven.

We are not aliens, praise God.

Ideal

Wisdom in supreme; therefore get wisdom. Though it cost all you have, get understanding. (Prov. 4:7)

Wisdom is an idealistic characteristic to petition God and apply to one's self. Wisdom seems almost extinct in the world today. How ideal is wisdom to you?

Lord, when you created us you had an ideal character in mind. I pray to be true to that vision. Jesus, I'm beginning to realize the reason for your purposes. You allow trials; they turn us to you in desperation, and the closer we are drawn to you, the closer becomes our personal relationship with you.

Lord, we are often as small children, are we not? I envisage a tiny child playing happily in the garden or the park, without a thought for her mother until she falls, and then she comes running to her for comfort and healing balm. Christians are frequently the same with you. We often go our merry way when all is well, but as soon as we face the fiery darts of the evil one and trouble comes upon us, we too come running to you. This too can be an idyllic situation, as whatever it takes to turn us to you is for our profit. Then again, I have noticed hardships can have the opposite effect; some turn against you and blame you in times of turmoil.

Jesus, the recent heartaches and the trials endured by my family over the last couple of months—such anguish. I would not call them ideal. However, you see all in a different light than do I. Your thoughts are high above my thoughts. In my morning devotions with you, you spoke of rejoicing at all times. The secret of doing so is trusting that you know the outcome. Lord, I must confess on occasion that I do resent trials and tribulations; Often I fail to see them as ideal.

> *My child, all go through fiery trials. It is your steadfastness that enables you to stand. Let nothing move you.*

I know Paul and his disciples agreed in Acts, "We must go through many hardships to enter the kingdom of God" (Acts 14:22). So I guess hardships are a training ground. Forgive me, Lord, as from time to time I break the commandment of "do not covet" when I envy those on the smooth and calm road. Assist me, please help me to let nothing move me and to find ways to praise you in the midst of trials and tribulations. Jesus, I'm in need of your assistance to surmount all the heartbreaking offenses before me. Please assist me to understand that these are tests—tests I will pass and overcome victoriously by your power.

Lord, you say, "The sacrifices of God are a broken spirit; a broken and contrite heart, O God, you will not despise" (Ps. 51:17). Your ways are as far as the east is from the west in relation to human reasoning. Thinking it through, Jesus, I realize that we need to come to you in brokenness. Whatever pleases you, my Lord, is idyllic. When self is in ascendancy, the Holy Spirit is limited in His achievements, because of our free will, which you will not infringe upon.

I dream of that day of release—the day when this vessel is broken, and the trials fade into oblivion. I recall you said not to expect trials to diminish but to increase, as the nearer I come to you the more ferocious the devil becomes. Lord, this will not affect me once I surrender all to you. It will be as water off a duck's back. Jesus, as this becomes fact, then the idyllic dream of mine will become reality.

You did say, Jesus, that we're all unique; as you created an ideal character in each individual, you work to bring to bloom these characteristics embedded within at conception. That is indeed idyllic; I give glory to you, my Lord.

> *My daughter, you are favored—not loved more, as I love all the same. But you are precious and chosen. As my child, you enjoy great benefits. The world's plagues will not touch you. Celebrate your uniqueness.*

Thank you, Lord! I stand so undeservingly. Your kind and loving words comfort me. I appreciate you will uphold and sustain me as I go through these extremely unfavorable conditions. I have no doubt I will grow into that ideal character planned by you. How magnificent, Jesus!

> *I have sustained you, and I will sustain you. But in all the adversities, in all the stumbling blocks that have been put before you, your greatest joy has been found in me, and that has been your sustaining portion.*

My praise I truly give you, Lord. You have sustained me; I'm not at the mercy of the man, fate, or the devil. I've felt such trepidation in adverse situations and apprehension in regard to the future, but I rise above them as I see your purpose behind them. I praise you, Father God, that you turn all hostile circumstance into ideal conditions. Heavenly Father, I ask you in Jesus' name, please assist me to learn both by suffering and by joy.

His divine power has given us everything we need for life and godliness through our knowledge of him who called us by his own glory and goodness. Through these he has given us his very great and precious promises, so that through them you may participate in the divine nature. (2 Pet. 1:3-4)

How ideal is this? Describe your response to these precious promises.

44

Your Purpose

Who, when he came, and had seen the grace of God, was glad, and exhorted them all, that with purpose of heart they would cleave unto the Lord. (Acts 11:23 KJV)

This is His purpose—to cleave to Him. Pray silently in your heart, thanking God for the unique purpose he has for your life.

My prayer, Lord, is for a peaceful life, void of trouble. This is what I crave, Jesus, but your Word says, "Consider it pure joy, my brothers, whenever you face trials of many kinds, because you know that the testing of your faith develops perseverance" (James 1:2–3). So this I do, Lord—I hope, without too much murmuring and complaint as I await your return.

I dare say, Jesus, I have been looking for pathways out of hardship instead of pathways into your kingdom. Lord, how impractical has this been? This has not been your intention. I've wasted energy being regretful of the way things are and longing for how they were. Jesus, I'm now conscious I've missed your purpose completely. This has not been your objective. Your purpose is to embrace these trials of abuse, malice, and hardship and welcome them as friends—to let go of animosity and instead consider them pure joy.

O Lord Jesus, this goes against the grain! I'm aware of what to do; it's the doing that's the difficult part. Please instill into my mind the verse that says I can do everything through him who gives me strength (Phil. 4:13). It shames me to think of the time taken to live up to this verse, and this desire, to date, has not been completely fulfilled. We all have such need of you. When all is surrendered into your hands, Jesus, and eyes, mind, and heart are focused on you, the mountains will not appear so overwhelming. All you allow is for a good purpose. Everything that comes into our life is to teach, rebuke, correct, and train, hence to grow into the righteousness of God and fulfill your objective. You Lord, our Creator, know exactly what is needed to bring each unique person into line with your vision, the path especially designed for each walk throughout this lifespan.

As I revisit the past, Jesus, I see these trials and hardships as exercises that strengthened and helped overcome hostility. Lord, you do give intermittent trouble-free living, and this is glorious. I can see the silver lining within. As I look upon hardships, I see them not as a sign of lacking your favor or being left to battle against the malicious forces alone, but as loving discipline that will better increase preparedness for spiritual warfare. When I dwell upon you, Lord, you become all-encompassing and paramount in my life. I love you, Jesus. I do so ramble on, but I'm sure it doesn't exasperate you.

Your purpose for us is to put you first. Wherever our main focus has been is our god. Sad to say, Lord, my focus till now has been upon regaining my normal life, to escape the trauma and strife endured. And yet, the comfort of the prior life does not train for battle! At this point, the normal life is exactly the life I'm now living. You revealed yesterday the previous life was one of avoiding unpleasantness and strife, holding fast to the predictable, and clutching tight to ease and comfort—as well as attaining wealth and social acceptability, and accumulating all manner of worldly things that are not evil in themselves but do not pertain to your goals, your purpose for me. The carnal life of the world, the life I yearned to return to, is not the normal life. It was an easy life, it was an easy way, but it was not your way, Jesus. This life I sought to return to did not have your blessing; it was not your intention! Whatever the reader's gods are, I wish to say, "The world's pleasures are only transitory. Jesus tells us to take up our cross and follow him." The cross is an instrument of crucifixion. It's there to crucify all that's ungodly within.

Lord, one objective of yours is for your people to introduce you to the lost. My walk with you has been both strange and wonderful. On the one hand, we invite people to come to you and ask them to hand their lives over to you, as you are the answer to all their problems. That's true—but afterward there is the other side of the coin: the discipline, testing, and training we need to go through to mature and become suitable for heaven. Then again, some are too busy in this world; they fail to give you a second glance. Many stay as spiritual babes.

Nonetheless, Jesus, you are the answer. Without you there is no prospect at all for mankind. Your purpose was set, Heavenly

Father. Jesus came of His own free will to suffer and die in our place.

Because of you, Jesus, billions are saved from damnation, those who claim you as their Savior, Lord, and Deliverer and are born again. For those baptized in the Spirit and with fire, there is a radiance, a joy that is inexpressible and a peace unexplainable. Jesus, I believe this joy for all your children has been your purpose too throughout the ages. All glory goes to you, Lord Jesus!

In him we were also chosen, having been predestined according to the plan of him who works out everything in conformity with the purpose of his will, in order that we, who were the first to hope in Christ, might be for the praise of his glory.
(Eph. 1:11–12)

Seek God's purpose for today. Record your praises to him here.

Radiant Light

And we have the word of the prophets made more certain, and you will do well to pay more attention to it, as to a light shining in a dark place, until the day dawns and the morning star rises in your hearts. (2 Peter 1:19)

Dwell upon this passage, seeking the brilliant, radiant light that emanates from Jesus.

Father, your radiant presence shines upon us as a precious gem. No matter what comes against us in the coming years, I pray we'll continue to shine your light. As it is said, "a new level, a new devil." But we pray to overcome—usually not without a battle, as the devil never gives up. He constantly seems to have a devious plan up his sleeve. Heavenly Father, whatever way he comes against your people, he's incapable to thwart you, our defender. You can defeat him with one word. He brings darkness and depression into hearts, but you, Lord, bestow radiant light.

To be certain, Jesus, it is not always beneficial to sidestep trials, as they are instrumental in teaching spiritual lessons. The hardship, training, and discipline that has been my portion over the years has developed my reliance and trust in you. I applaud you, Lord, as I am now finally able to see through the suffering and darkness into your brilliant light; consequently, this causes my heart to rejoice.

> *My precious daughter, the light that shines upon you will keep you on the right path. Where I send you, you are to go without question. I love you and wish for you happiness unknown to the world but known only to those who give their all-in love and praise to me. Do not turn away from the light; I am the light of the world. Stay your eyes upon me, my child. Not all see this radiant light from above, but pray that multitudes will in the time to come. Rest in my love, my child.*

Thank you, Jesus; there is much to bring joy within our lives. Lord, I love the resplendent lyrical praises King David sings to you in Scripture, "O LORD, our Lord, how majestic is your name in all the earth! You have set your glory above the heavens. . . . When I consider your heavens the work of your fingers, the moon and stars, which you have set in place, what is man that you are mindful of him, the son of man that you care for him?" (Ps. 8:1, 3–4). I remind myself, Lord, that life is not all trials and tribulations! It's been an exhilarating and adventurous journey, and for the most part a joyous and radiant one. At these times, trials fade into forgetfulness. The journey I've walked with you has developed into a closer friendship, one that's pleasurable and congenial.

My daughter, I too enjoy the pleasure you give me. Always keep looking to me, not to the world, for your happiness.

I know true and lasting happiness is not found in the world. Worldly happiness is fleeting; happiness and the joy gained from you is eternal. My heart is overwhelmed with joy at present, Lord. I view a flock of birds flying above, so free and graceful in flight. Merely to watch and listen to your creation bestows a feeling of peace and tranquility, just as the magnificence of a radiant sunset warms our hearts. It's good, dear Jesus, to be at one with nature. Seeing you in nature and knowing you are at all times present is such a delight. That takes away the stresses and turmoil of this world and the ache I experience in my heart for mankind. The changes our societies are moving toward are veering away from this brilliant light, the light of you, Lord Jesus.

Child, do not be troubled with the problems of the world; that is for my shoulders. I have a wonderful future for you. This does not mean you will never encounter trials. It is in trials that you grow to maturity; without them you would become shallow and self-centered, without empathy for others or love for me. You would think of yourself as self-sufficient and in need of nothing. Your need is what drives you to me.

I seek to live wholly for you, Jesus, whatever the cost. If that cost is to struggle through sufferings and turmoil, so be it. If through this journey the things and ways of this world are cast aside, and the radiant light together with a cherished relationship results, then it's all worthwhile. I would not exchange my communion with you, Lord Jesus, for all the relief of hardships in the world. You said, "I have told you all things, so that in me you may have peace. In this world you will have trouble. But take heart! I have overcome the world" (John 16:33). I do so take heart, Lord, and thank you for the meaningful life of joy and peace you give. No matter Satan's attempts to dim this radiant light in our lives, his darkness cannot cloud it out.

Such a glorious morning, Jesus; I take breakfast outdoors and enjoy the fresh air. I think of your creativity—it frequently astounds me. I marvel at the exquisiteness of the flowers, the bougainvillea's brilliant color, the fragrance of the rose, the harmony in a bird's song, the radiance of sunlight on the shimmering lake, the warmth of the sun, and the silvery light of the moon. For all this I give glory to you, Almighty God. You created this world and the beauty in nature for all to enjoy, no matter whether they do or do not accept you as Creator.

As I write to you, I am tempted to sit and bask in your presence and laze around enjoying the warmth of the day. But then I see little ants scurrying along in formation, intent on their business. What are they thinking? Do they think? It's great to relax, indulge myself, and enjoy your presence, but I must arouse and take a leaf out of the little ants' book and attend to business. Praise be to you, most glorious, radiant, Almighty God!

I have come into the world as a light, so no one who believes in me should stay in darkness. (John 12:46)

Dwell upon the significance of this light and jot down your thoughts.

Second Coming

Behold, I am coming soon! (Rev 22:7)

For as lightning that comes from the east is visible even in the west, so will be the coming of the Son of Man. (Matt. 24:27)

At that time they will see the Son of Man coming in a cloud with power and great glory. (Luke 21:27)

Jesus the Messiah is coming soon! Deliberate upon these words, and ponder them deep within your heart.

Lord Jesus, I look forward to the age of righteousness where peace and joy covers the world. Throughout your Word, Lord, it speaks of your second coming.

Likewise, I've been long watching and waiting for the rapture, but unsure if I'm ready.

> *Child, I want you to know that I have been guiding you daily, and you have been following. This time is all-important, as I want you to go ahead and tell those who will listen of my imminent return. You do not know how soon, but be ready, watching, and waiting. You have been trained by me, and I tell you that the only way you can go is up. This I say to comfort you and to let you know that all is under my control.*

Jesus, my heart overflows with love for you. Your words truly console me. I sincerely thank you and praise you and trust you totally! I wait for your imminent return, and I look forward to the millennial reign and beyond—a time when sin is eradicated and justice and peace reign. I look forward to the redemption of my body when raised incorruptible. How I relish the thought, to dwell with you for all eternity.

> *My child, this is a time when we should see great things happen. Walk in the light as one who is waiting for the time when I am to come. Sit with me a while and enjoy my presence. I protect and guide you always. This is not the world you live in; live always with me above.*

What an exciting time! I pray people will look up and will not be as the foolish virgins, but be astute as to the times we are living in. When you come for your bride, we must be pure and spotless. I trust, Jesus, that by the Holy Spirit you will empower us to wait patiently for the rapture (in case it occurs first) and be ready for this most captivating moment. Jesus, we are living through a darkened age but also an exciting time, as we see many Bible prophecies taking place. The rapture could occur at any moment. Then we shall be caught up in the air to meet you. This so excites, but at the same time my heart is heavy to think of those who will be left behind.

Lord, Christians hold differing opinions. For some there is no rapture; others have different timetables—pre-, mid-, post- I've heard of a couple others recently, pre-wrath and partial rapture. This is all irrelevant. It is nobler to wait, watch, and be ready for you, Lord, whenever you do come. First Thessalonians 4:16–18 speaks of being caught in the clouds to meet you in the air. Some Christians say these verses refer to the second coming, but I don't understand. Jesus, how can this be, as when you come the second time you come to the earth (not only in the clouds) and the millennial rule will commence? Jesus, no one knows the day or hour when the rapture will occur, and it is foolishness to set dates, but it will unquestionably be the most electrifying moment of our lives! I'm certain it will be so for you too, Jesus.

My dear child, I have been working toward this momentous occasion down through the ages.

Jesus, in Old Testament times, many Israelites yearned for your first coming, their long-predicted deliverer, their messiah. In this age of grace, we also look forward with joy to your second coming. Jesus, you showed me a vision: I saw you walking hurriedly through the pastures under the trees with your disciples at dusk. I could hear the twigs crackling under your feet. I heard the urgency in your voice as you said, "We must work while it is still day, for night comes when no one can work" (see John 9:4). Lord, I suspect we have little time remaining.

> *Child, keep your eyes on me and your ears attuned to me, and you will not miss the trumpet call.*

Lord Jesus, to miss the trumpet call would be the most terrifying and ominous situation to find ourselves in. I look forward to your return with excitement and joy.

> The glory of your appearance
> The sweetness of embrace
> Lovely beyond description
> Is our Lord Jesus' depiction
> He overflows with joy and generates grace
> As we await the rapture to see his face.

For the Lord himself will come down from heaven, with a loud command, with the voice of the archangel and with the trumpet call of God, and the dead in Christ will rise first. After that, we who are still alive and are left will be caught up together with them in the clouds to meet the Lord in the air. And so we will be with the Lord forever. Therefore encourage each other with these words. (1 Thess. 4:16–18)

What expectations do you have from this significant occasion?

Will you inform and encourage others in regard to this noteworthy time?

Urgency

This is a momentous time in the history of man.

The urgency is for all to be ready and awaiting his arrival.

Are you ready?

Not only must we be ready for your coming, Lord, but we must also work to bring others into the kingdom. Your hurried steps in the vision and the urgency in your voice indicate the nearness of the end of this age. The dusk indicates we are moving into darkness. Does that indicate the tribulation? I can see by the atrocities occurring worldwide that the powers of darkness are powerfully at work.

My child, please tell my children to be ready for a complete breakdown of the world's system. This is a prophecy from Daniel; it is near at hand. I say to all my people who will listen, be ready for me and my angels, my heavenly helpers. I will come for my own with all the might and power of the universe. Be watching and waiting, for the night is coming.

Jesus, I consider you are speaking of the rapture—or is it your second coming? No matter, Lord; we need to prepare. I see economic problems among the nations, weather catastrophes, and violence occurring worldwide.

Go, my daughter, slowly and with deliberation, to tell those of the time now approaching. It is the greatest time of all for people who are being saved.

And Lord, turbulent times for those who are not! As we watch for your return, I can see much that is prophesied in your Word coming to pass. We must keep up with ancient biblical prophecies and live our lives according to your Word, and all will be well.

Jesus, you referred to the signs of the end of the age in Luke: "There will be signs in the sun, moon and stars. On the earth, nations will be in anguish and perplexity at the roaring and tossing of the sea" (Luke 21:25). The last sentence sounds like a tsunami. You could speak one word to stop all this; you are Lord over nature. Lord, I'm of the opinion that man is not entirely the cause of climate change. I believe that everything happening is an urgent wake-up call from you, that you *are* God and you *are* coming back. So, it is crucial to ready ourselves. First Thessalonians speaks about your return, as does Matthew. Matthew speaks of earthquakes as the beginning signs of the end of this age, and all must come to pass before your return. Lord, there has been an alarming spike in major earthquakes in recent decades—in fact, an explosion in numbers.

With the excitement of your return there is another aspect, the other side of the coin, the great tribulation. Matthew states, "There will be great distress, unequaled from the beginning of the world until now and never to be equaled again. If those days had not been cut short no one would survive, but for the sake of the elect those days will be shortened" (Matt. 24:21–22). Almighty God, thank you for that promise, that you will return before we annihilate ourselves. It is you and only you that can save! Man's attempt to decrease carbon emission is futile, as it is you who controls the weather.

Jesus, the world is approaching an extremely crucial time of decision. Satan knows his time is short, and is working relentlessly to deceive multitudes before his demise. But Lord, I appreciate you will deliver all who are ready from the hour of destruction as promised. Jesus, born-again and Spirit-baptized Christians have been given authority and been empowered by you, our Lord and Savior, to destroy the works of the devil. But non-Christians don't hold that authority; also, Satan has blinded many to the truth. You, my Lord, warned of the times to come and the urgency for all to come into your kingdom to escape the fiery pit. Please give me the words to warn and urge those who go their own way without a thought of the approaching storm. I pray, please open the eyes Satan has closed. I pray they will invite you to do this, as you will not violate their gift of free will.

My child, I love you deeply. This will be a time of desperation on the part of those who trust in their own understanding. You should be endeavoring to tell the world who you are by your actions and peaceful life. This is your opportunity to spread the gospel. All things I say to you, pass on! Help others share in the glory I have for my own. I tell you, you are blessed beyond all you can imagine. I love you, so go in peace.

All of this is both good and bad news—good for those who are being saved and not so good for those who are not. In fact, it's horrifying. I pray those who have been deceived, pacified, and hushed to sleep by Satan to become alert to the danger and urgency within their lives—to flee from what is about to befall them.

I will show you my intentions. I will trust you to tell others and prepare them. Now go and tell what is going to happen to the ungodly of this world, and how those who do not consider me but who say they are mine will finish up.

O my Lord, this is bad news—nevertheless, good news is coming for all who love you.

We all need empowerment to witness as we see these times approaching.

There is an urgency to do so before it's too late. Are you prepared?

Judgment

He will judge the world in righteousness; he will govern the peoples with justice. (Ps. 9:8)

With this in view, what is your observation on God's righteousness and his judgments? Think upon these things.

Father God, I bring to you Christians who say they belong to you but do not. I fear for them and pray for them, that they will awaken from their dangerous state, arouse from their slumber, diligently seek a devoted relationship with you, refrain from giving you merely lip service, and hereafter gain a love that is pure and holy. I plead for loved ones; I pray they will be ready with joy to receive you before the rapture. I ask this in Jesus' precious name. Heavenly Father, we are in exciting times, yet I discern change is coming as you inform the nations you're unhappy with their disbelief and the moral landside in regard to your holy laws.

The atrocities that have been executed against Christians in Muslim and other lands where millions of Christians are killed and executed in all manner of gruesome ways—this grieves me as it must grieve you. They have not been given the authorization to judge who is to live and who is to die. You set the times of our earthly lives on this earth. These people have assumed your authority. It is for you to judge, Jesus. I pray most of all for sinners and those who sit on the fence to repent and come into a loving friendship with you. If not, they may hear these terrifying words at the judgment seat: "I never knew you. Away from me, you evildoers!" (Matt. 7:23). Oh, my Lord, that would be the worst thing my ears could ever hear!

What will you find Lord, when you return—in these final times that many call "the enlightened age," a deceptive delusion from Satan? Today we make laws to protect snakes, but then pass draconian laws to kill babes in the womb, and this is "enlightenment"! Lord, most biblical prohibitions that governments are inept to deal with, they legalize. In this so-called progressive age, it is now not a problem.

It is urgent for all Christians to speak out against laws made in opposition to your holy laws. We see riots and wars; we see the destruction of human life. We have instituted laws to enable people to sign their own death warrants, naming it euthanasia. This scares me, Lord. Euthanasia is a slippery slope, yet many people are crying out for it. It is you who has determined our years upon this earth. We see the devaluing of marriage to suit gay couples; and Lord, children are told in this so-called "enlightened age" that they can determine their own sex. It is you, Jesus, who create and determine the sexes. You are our God and Creator, but the reverence, worship, and the love you deserve is lacking lately in my country. Your name, Jesus, is a curse word to many. This lack of respect for traditional values and Christian beliefs are all repugnant to you. I trust you have been shaking nations with natural disasters to wake up and call out to you in repentance. All that is needed is the cry of sincere repentance and acceptance of you, Jesus, to rescue us and save us from this fallen world and the final judgment.

Our nation is legalizing behaviors you speak against in Scripture, and many of our leaders have no fear of you. Many are blinded to the truth and happy to believe the lie. The Scripture said, "The god of this age has blinded the minds of unbelievers" (2 Cor. 4:4). I'm afraid for these people and I pray for them, as they do not know that judgment is coming. Unaware, they walk the broad way to damnation. No matter their attempts to shroud the truth, truth cannot be hidden or silenced. One day we will all approach the judgment seat and then realize that you, Jesus, are the eternal Judge and that no one can hide from you. I pray they will not be too late to seek you. Lord, I ask the Holy Spirit to speak into the lives of family, friends, and acquaintances, some that are clever at blanketing truth. My hope is that they will look to you before your return and refuse to take the mark of the beast; if they welcome it, they will then belong to Satan. Lord, I hope against hope they will delve into your Word, as it is our standard of judgment in both physical and spiritual issues.

Lord Jesus, I entreat those who read this book and are in need of redemption to make a 180-degree turnabout and not live as the world lives, but by every word that comes from the Bible, the Word of God.

Lord Jesus, you desire all to come into your kingdom, where your love is everlasting and where you have prepared a mansion for each person. My prayer is they will open their minds, open their ears, hear the message of the cross and the resurrection, and come to a belief in you, repent of their sins, and accept you and the sacrifice you made at Calvary on their behalf.

Lord, I ask you to accept my repentance, too. My heart is torn when I see people harden their hearts and minds against you. On the day of judgment when we all must face you, how terrible it will be for those who do not know you! And how jubilant for those who do, those who have had a true conversion! What a glorious day that will be! I pray many of my family and friends will come to the valley of decision before your return and decide to put their lives into your hands and their destiny into heaven.

My daughter, do not be concerned about what is to come. This is an important time in the history of humanity. I will tell you all you need to know. Wait upon me, listen and obey. This I cannot stress too much.

Jesus, I'm exceedingly concerned for those who do not have a close relationship with you. My prayer is they will see that judgment is coming, and that they will get into your Word and become aware of the time we are living in.

For it is time for judgment to begin with the family of God; and if it begins with us, what will the outcome be for those who do not obey the gospel of God? (1 Pet. 4:17)

Are you ready for the judgment, however and whenever it comes?

Think about what you have observed on this subject.

The Word

Let the word of Christ dwell in you richly as you teach and admonish one another with all wisdom, and as you sing psalms, hymns and spiritual songs with gratitude in your hearts to God. (Col. 3:16)

God's Word is enlightening; as we learn Scripture, it becomes alive deep within our hearts. How would you describe this scripture?

Father God, this evening I thank you for the Bible, your precious book—for every page, for every promise contained therein, for its principles, predictions, and the mighty revelation of Lord Jesus Christ. In it, we can discover the truth. The Bible is truly a story of rescue. The Holy Scriptures bring to us the story of you, Jesus the Messiah, who came with love and grace to rescue us from the dominion of darkness and sin.

Lord, your Word is printed on our hearts; we are without excuse, we are given a choice. We are set free to trust you and surrender all. The word "gospel" means good news, and the best news is to know you, Jesus, as Lord and Savior. The most precious experience is to be led by you into a loving relationship. Nothing is of any consequence except you and your life within. My desire, Lord, is for all who read the Bible to see the underlying meaning and the deeper spiritual issues within the Scriptures, not only to skim the surface.

You are the Word, Lord Jesus, the living Word. I pray, Jesus, that as we all deliberate upon your words and apply them to our lives, they may sink deep within our hearts. Jesus, many in this so-called "confident age" are confident that they are safe and nothing can touch them. They turn a blind eye to the fact of the judgment; they deny the inerrancy of Scripture and deny it is the inspired Word of God. Many pseudo-Christians do so as well. I believe you cannot lie and your word is truth. No one has been able to come up with evidence that it is not, though many have tried. Furthermore, there are verses in the Scriptures that validate the truth of the inspired Word of God. We must have faith that you are God or believe you are a liar and a fraud. Jesus, I believe in God the Father, God the Son, and God the Holy Spirit!

Lord, those who do not have the Scriptures can see you through nature, the wonders of your creative work. Lord, I thank you for your *rhema* word, the word you speak that is spiritually perceived. Still again I thank you for your Holy Spirit who reveals the deep truths of the Bible. Your biblical promises, Lord, are the most trustworthy truths ever. Praise you, Heavenly Father, for the wonderful gift of your son Jesus, who has revealed to us your likeness and has taught us how to live godly lives as you ordained before the foundation of the world.

Every day, Lord, I realize more and more the importance of staying in prayer and the study of Scripture, as evil spirits are in an all-out war to strip us of these benefits. Satan is a defeated foe and can be defeated by the powerful Word of God. You, Jesus, overcame Satan with Scripture when you were tempted during your forty days in the wilderness. I pray we all may do likewise.

I endeavor with your assistance to dig deep into your Word, as your truth is given in multilevel layers. By a diligent search for the treasures hidden there, truth is revealed; and when acted upon, spiritual growth is enhanced. Father God, I pray in Jesus' name that the citizens of this country will be alert to the times. You are doing a new thing, and I ask Christians to come out of this world and immerse themselves in your precious Word! This world offers nothing of eternal worth.

Jesus, as I read the Bible, I see that each prophet has a piece, a component which illuminates specific ideas about you and your truth. Your Holy Spirit increases our understanding, which allows us to know you in a deeper sense. In you, Jesus, we can see the exact likeness of God our Father. You are the truth, and as we seek for the whole truth, we are freed. I see, Jesus, that it is imperative to keep in the Word and live by its directives, and not worship the false gods of wealth, fame, sports, movie stars, science, technology, family, or even self. Jesus, in the light of your love and in the mighty power of your Word, whatever you desired you had only to speak and it came into being. The insignificant, impotent gods the modern world worships today are what keep many away from you, Jesus, and from heaven.

I choose to meditate on your Word. How can I explain your Word, Jesus? Your Word is more precious than any treasure trove of jewels. Your Word is our final authority; Jesus, it is vital to judge all by Scripture. I pray to speak a word that others may see the silver lining within. Solomon explained words quite fittingly in Proverbs: "A word aptly spoken is like apples of gold in pictures of silver" (Prov. 25:11, KJV). I hope many will see you throughout Scripture, Jesus, and rejoice. I pray your words will be the meditation of our hearts day and night.

And we also thank God continually because, when you received the word of God, which you heard from us, you accepted it not as the word of men, but as it actually is, the word of God, which is at work in you who believe.
(1 Thess. 2:13)

When you walk in the light of Jesus and accept his word, a beautiful transformation occurs within. Consider the words of Paul above, and pen your reaction to them.

Worldwide Fellowship

We proclaim to you what we have seen and heard, so that you also may have fellowship with us. And our fellowship is with the Father, and with his son, Jesus Christ. We write this to make our joy complete. (1 John 1:3-4)

What significance to you is the fellowship of Jesus, Christians, and other people in your life?

Contemplate this topic.

Jesus, it's a joy to converse with you and discuss your Word with other Christians and enjoy their fellowship. You say, "For where two or three come together in my name, there am I with them" (Matt. 18:20). Delightful!

My daughter, it is lovely to hear you discussing My Word and fellowshipping together with Me. It is a joy to My heart. My people don't realize what a joy it brings to My heart, or the need that I too have for companionship with you. I love you all; I hear you, and I will answer your prayers.

How beautiful, Lord—I've forever thought that you, being omnipotent, would have need of nothing. Yet the Bible states, "God is love" (1 John 4:16). It is clear that love should be reciprocated. Therefore, Lord, the need is real in this respect. Your appeal is for our love; that's it, isn't it? Unquestionably, Father God, your preference is for a family—why else would you create us in your image? Why else would you call us your children? Your desire is for our companionship. As we enjoy sweet fellowship together in your presence, it is an indisputable fact that we bring you joy. It's not only Christians whose company and friendship you desire, but with all races and religions, as your love magnifies itself and spreads equally upon the entire world.

Lord, I imagine the restraint it must take not to exercise your power to produce love in all. You, who can command a universe, restrain yourself as far as we humans are concerned because of our free will; our love must be freely given. You do not want robots. I've been pondering the reason the Israelites lost fellowship with you. What you desire, Heavenly Father, is rapport with all your created ones; your wish is to call all back to you. It's harmony you look for in your creation, is that not so, Jesus? Man's attempts at creating unity fall far short of perfection, and sometimes the result can be catastrophic.

There is no better example of man's failure to unite and live in harmony and fellowship than the Palestinian-Israeli situation. I fear this is a spiritual war and am afraid that peace will not be obtained by human effort but only by you. Then we shall have utopia. Jesus, I've been reflecting on the history of the Promised Land. I believe the Israelites lost fellowship with you because of their disobedience, which contributed to their dispersion throughout the world. Also, the Arabs would have known you as descendants of Abraham, but they too lost fellowship with you, Heavenly Father, somehow along the way and turned to another god.

Your promise was that the Israelis would return, never again to be uprooted; and as prophesied, they have returned after almost two millennia and resettled their ancient homeland. Jesus, the Jewish return was truly miraculous, although this has caused much controversy and discord among the Palestinians, the Arab nations, and much of the world. I appeal to you, Jesus, that you will impress upon these peoples' minds to recall history. Lord, the Jews are the apple of your eye, whom you desire to fellowship with. I undoubtedly see your hand in the miracle of the Israelis' return after two thousand years of dispersion.

Jesus, the wars instigated against them have been won against all odds. It's unquestionable that you saved this malaria-infested swamp, and Jerusalem their capital, for the Jewish return. Through the Jews' hard work and innovative genius, they have turned this desolate land into the thriving country it is today in less than seventy years. This has not been a peaceful resettlement; surrounding nations and many other countries throughout the world war against it. So, it is true, nothing is new! Scripture says Sanballat, Geshem the Arab, and other enemies were scheming against Nehemiah when they returned from the Babylonian captivity to rebuild the city walls. The Arabs thousands of years ago were unable to fellowship with the Israelis, and today are still fighting against the Jewish people, attempting to prevent them from rebuilding. Sadly, human nature has not changed. No fellowship, no friendship. I dare say King Solomon was right: "What has been will be again, what has been done will be done again; there is nothing new under the sun" (Eccl. 1:9).

Lord, I pray against the decadent faceless people around the world who spew their repulsive perverted posts against Israel on social media. These people contribute to the disharmony between the two. Is it possible that these faceless people will put their hate behind them, as it's destructive to peace, and instead reach out in fellowship? I also long for the inhabitants of our world to love each other and fellowship together. We are all humans created in your image. Jesus, there is too much hate in the world. Hate hurts, hate is destructive to companionship, hate destroys; hate tears down, hate manifests in cruelty!

Child, love is the greatest weapon; it is love that builds up. My child, keep near to me in continued fellowship, and you will be kept safe from the deceiver.

I give praises to you, Lord Jesus. The Scriptures say to pray for the peace of Jerusalem, so I pray for Jerusalem. I thank you for your protection of the Israeli nation and pray that you will regain fellowship with your chosen people.

I love this verse, Jesus: "Whatever is true, whatever is noble, whatever is right, whatever is pure, whatever is lovely, whatever is admirable—if anything is excellent or praiseworthy—think about such things" (Phil. 4:8). How glorious, a divine verse! How great it would be if we all could live our lives and keep our thoughts upon these exquisite words. I marvel, Almighty God, that you are so taken up with puny man. Your desire is to fellowship and commune with your created ones. Jesus, I pray once more for all who read this to seek a connection to you, to follow you and create a relationship with you. Jesus, to sit with you and enjoy your friendship is the most idyllic relationship on this earth.

If we walk in the light, as he is in the light, we have fellowship with one another, and the blood of Jesus, his son, purifies us from all sin. (1 John 1:7)

How does this verse enrich your knowledge of God?

Praise

Through Jesus, therefore, let us continually offer to God a sacrifice of praise—the fruit of lips that confess his name.
(Heb. 13:15)

Can you imagine what transformation it would make to your prayer life and relationship with Jesus if it was one of continual praise?

Jesus, you are altogether lovely! You reveal yourself in *shekinah* glory. To know you is to love you, and to love you is to praise you. I pour out my praises to you and worship you, Almighty God. I would have been long defeated without the ability to praise. Praise has been the only factor, the only way of survival. Singing praises to you,

Jesus, lifts us out of this world into the spiritual realm. Dear Jesus, you are the only one in this entire universe who would put up with my tuneless voice.

Child, praise me often—worship and love me. Live close to me, and the power of praise will flow from you wherever you are.

As I read your Word, I see how the elders in heaven are constantly praising you, singing, "You are worthy, our Lord and God, to receive glory and honor and power, for you created all things, and by your will they were created and have their being" (Rev. 4:11). Jesus, the angels, the elders, and every living being in heaven praises you. "Worthy is the Lamb, who was slain, to receive power and wealth and wisdom and strength and honor and glory and praise!" (Rev. 5:12). Jesus, you truly are praiseworthy.

Lord, I love the sound of your Hebrew name, *Yeshua*. The name "Jesus" has repeatedly been used blasphemously; it stings the Christian heart whenever it is uttered in that manner. Surely it must grieve you too, my Lord. I long for the day when we shall all join together in heaven and worship with the heavenly beings. Lord Jesus, you are sovereign and so majestic, yet so tender and gracious. I do appreciate you, Lord, for you invested your very life in your creation. My prayer is that I may reflect more and more of your joy, that joy that pervades all heaven in dazzling splendor. You alone are worthy of glorification and worship. Lord, you're not only the God of Israel; you are the universal God. You died, Lord Jesus, not only for the Israelites but for all nations. As the psalmist said, "Praise be to the LORD

God, the God of Israel, who alone does marvelous deeds. Praise be to his glorious name forever; may the whole earth be filled with your glory. Amen and Amen" (Ps. 72:18–19). Lord, it is praise that brings the glory of God down, is it not?

Praise is a powerful weapon against Satan and his demons—and a term of endearment for you, Lord, and my family and friends. I give you my adoration, dear Jesus, for the sacrifice and the enormous suffering you endured on our behalf. I can imagine the mammoth effort it took for you to exercise self-control to hang there on the cross. Man could not kill you; it was the Father's will. It was out of love for this fallen world that you hung on that excruciatingly painful cross, so that we who believe would attain eternal life and spend eternity in your bright and beautiful home forever!

Lord, I'm sorry; I can barely stop myself. I'm so passionate about you, even obsessive, as I go on and on each time I dwell on your sacrifice and resurrection. I imagine you have assignments and all kinds of employments in your kingdom for your children, tasks designed and adapted individually for each soul, work that gives joy and delight in the undertaking. I exalt you, Lord; I revere and worship you, because you are my shepherd. The psalmist said, "The Lord is my shepherd, I shall not be in want. He makes me lie down in green pastures, he leads me beside quiet waters, he restores my soul" (Ps. 23:1–3). This verse, Lord, gives a vision of peace. And in that peace, I praise you for the healing and abundant life that comes from you.

I thank you, my Lord Jesus, and I praise you that you reveal yourself in Scripture and personally. As I perceive your omnipotence, I see you as the Supreme God and Sovereign Lord. We are all undeserving of your love and attention. My sense of unworthiness tends to make me hold back as I stand in awe of you.

Jesus, at other times, I forget I am speaking to Almighty God—I see you as my friend and just ramble on about everything and nothing. I thank you, God Almighty, that you work tirelessly for each of your children and also for those who at present do not know you. Your love embraces each equally with a love that transcends the human mind. Humans are so imperfect and frail in comparison to you who is perfect and invincible. You're the one of importance; you are the supreme, most powerful being in the universe. It's difficult to comprehend why you would bother with me, a lowly person who all would pass by in the street without a second glance—a nonentity. Yet you come, Almighty God, at my slightest call. Often, Lord, I'm so overcome with wonderment and reverence for you that I succumb to tears of joy. This engenders a feeling of adoration, Jesus; I adore you and wish to praise you continually.

Lord, you are so meek, kind, gentle, and loving. In those moments, it's difficult to imagine you as Sovereign Lord, God Almighty. Lord Jesus, you know all about me. You know each thought, each motive, so I suspect it's a little ludicrous telling you what you already know. My childishness is to some extent foolishness, but you have not chided me for it, so I expect you don't mind.

My child, I enjoy listening. I am interested in all you say, and you are not childish; you are precious in my sight.

Thank you, Jesus. You fill me with joy and happiness. I see now that there's no need to apologize for rambling. I am so conscious of my own fragility, but in you I am strong. In this I praise you, my Lord. Hallelujah!

When he came near the place where the road goes down the Mount of Olives, the whole crowd of disciples began joyfully to praise God in loud voices for all the miracles they had seen: "Blessed is the king who comes in the name of the Lord!" "Peace in heaven and glory in the highest!"
(Luke 19:37–38)

What does this verse disclose about your God? Compose your thoughts below.

Happiness

Where there is no vision, the people perish: but he who keepeth the law, happy is he. (Prov. 29:18 KJV)

"I will rejoice in the Lord, I will be joyful in God my Savior. (Hab. 3:18)

Envisage the direction you wish to proceed in your Christian walk.

Pray for the joy that comes from God, the joy no one can take away.

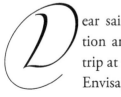ear saints, come with me. Bring your imagination and let it run wild. Dream of the ultimate trip at the end of your journey through this earth. Envisage that mighty leap into the heavens, and

the walk along the golden streets in pristine glistening light, the joyous homecoming. The happiness felt as you see Jesus, and your family and relatives who have gone on before excitedly welcoming you to your mansion—where keys and locks are not needed, as no thief will break in; where there is neither a clock nor a watch to be seen, nor frantic racing against time as today, since we'll live in a timeless zone for all eternity; a place where you can sit quietly with Jesus in true humility; eternally in his presence; where his love overwhelms you in happiness and joy. How great will that be? Never, ever more to depart!

My children, this gives me such joy, I can barely bridge the gap until this becomes reality. Sit quietly and keep watching for that day, my children.

Lord Jesus, inasmuch as I am seated in your presence, my sadness turns to joy; you surround me with happiness. There's no comparison between the marvels of the world and your joy in the human heart. I praise you for the strength given to triumph over the evil one's trials brought against my family and me. Now I can rise above all Satan's hostility, and above all my frailty and timidity.

I give you my adoration for your discipline and your correction. Your love, which persisted through times of struggle and resistance on my part, has enabled me now to appreciate what I once thought was harshness on your part. Truly it was love and only love that kept you bringing me back these many years to the point of letting go and letting God. Your love within overcomes all strife encountered throughout life on earth. It's beyond magnificent, beyond marvelous for the human language to express, just complete happiness.

I regret my remark the other day, Lord, that I was a nonentity. You certainly do not create insignificant people. All the billions created by you, Lord, are outstandingly remarkable; we are all precious in your sight. So I'm not a nobody. My Father is the King of the Universe; therefore, I am a princess. Hallelujah! Lord, I believe heaven to be a place of indescribable happiness. Jesus, I look forward to the joy of seeing you face to face on arrival. I would love to put on the garment of praise and walk with you on the golden streets, or race with you to determine how fast I can run on my renewed legs—or even dance with you. Do you dance? King David liked to dance on earth, and I am pretty sure he would do so in heaven.

> *My precious girl, I would love to dance with you. It would be a great joy.*

My Lord, my Jesus, you are so glorious! I believe wherever you are is heaven, whether it be on the new earth or new heaven. Really, Lord, you are omnipresent. As I contemplate the loveliness of heaven, I dream of the day when I can walk with you, when "there will be no more death or mourning or crying or pain, for the old order of things has passed away. . . . Nothing impure will ever enter it, nor will anyone who does what is shameful and deceitful, but only those whose names are written in the Lamb's book of life" (Rev. 21:4, 27).

Glory, Jesus, all who love you will live in a place of indefinable beauty and radiance, where the environment is clean and pure, where happiness, music, love, and joy is in the air. Lord, I envisage earth to be in some ways similar to heaven. Only the earth is flawed; we humans are to blame for our lack of righteous control. Heaven is so much vaster and beyond all imagination for human words to express. What a grand surprise and a joyous occasion when we all arrive there for the wedding feast. We will then be able to say, "The kingdom of the world has become the kingdom of our Lord and of his Christ, and He will reign forever and ever" (Rev. 11:15). Hallelujah! Amen! What a wondrous time this will be! I love you, Lord Jesus!

My child, I too wait for the completion of all things, when we can all live in joy, peace, and harmony in heaven for eternity. Work toward this momentous occasion.

Praise be to you, mighty God and sovereign Lord!
How great you are!

Endnotes

1. Frances J. Roberts, *Come Away My Beloved* (Uhlrichsville, OH: Barbour Publishing, 2002), 230.
2. "Two Listeners," *God Calling*, ed. A. J. Ruddell, Australian edition (Kippa-Ring, Queensland, Australia: CLC Australasia, 2010), 243.
3. James Allen, *As a Man Thinketh* (Ilfracombe, England: Collins, London and Glasgow, n.d.), 35.
4. E. M. Bounds, *Power through Prayer* (Chicago: Moody, 1979), 14–15.
5. Bill Yount, *I Heard Heaven Proclaim* (Hagerstown, MD: McDougal Publishing, 2004), 96–97.
6. Dick Eastman, *The Hour That Changes the World* (Grand Rapids, MI: Baker Book House, 1978), 11.
7. Ibid., 14.
8. Marie Shropshire, *In Touch with God* (Eugene, OR: Harvest House Publishers, 1985), 43.
9. Eastman, *The Hour That Changes the World*, 78.
10. Bounds, *Power through Prayer*, 10.
11. Eastman, *The Hour That Changes the World*, 9.
12. Bounds, *Power through Prayer*, 44.
13. Roberts, *Come Away My Beloved*, 27.

14. Sarah Young, *Jesus Calling: A 365 Day Journaling Devotional* (Nashville: Thomas Nelson, 2010), Nov. 24.
15. "Two Listeners," *God Calling*, 274.
16. Ibid., 89.
17. Young, *Jesus Calling*, Mar. 5.

Acknowledgments

I wish to express my appreciation for the Deep River Books team.

Special thanks to Bill Carmichael and Andy Carmichael, the Publishers. Bill was kindness itself, and Andy showed unbelievable patience with this first-time author for whom publishing was as daunting as a trip to the moon.

I am indebted to Sean Tosello, who tended to my queries in an exceptionally obliging nature. Also to Carl Simmons, who edited *Purify My Heart* and provided formatting suggestions. To Tamara Barnet, who oversaw the editing and coordinated the design and printing process, thanks—it looks terrific.

I am so grateful for my friend Doris Thobaven, who was the first to set eyes on this manuscript to proofread before sending it to the editor.

Last, but not least, I wish to express my gratitude to Rachel Starr Thomson, who performed the first edit and came up with the beautiful title and made it possible for this book to be published.

I pray God's blessing upon you all.

Printed in Australia
AUHW011130031120
336564AU00001B/1